THE FAMILY CREATIVE WORKSHOP

1

Acrylics, Afghan Stitch, Airplanes of Paper, American Indian Crafts, Animal Dolls, Ant Farms, Antiquing Furniture, Applique, Astronomy, Baby Foods, Basketry, Batik

Plenary Publications International, Inc.
New York and Amsterdam

On the cover
Cowhide oiled with neat's-foot oil, a scratch awl,
rawhide stitching. See the American Indian leather
moccasins project on page 42.
Photograph by Paul Levin.

Published by Plenary Publications International,
Incorporated, 300 East 40th Street, New York, N.Y. 10016,
for the Blue Mountain Crafts Council.

Library of Congress Catalog Card Number: 73-89331.
Complete set International Standard Book Number:
0-88459-021-6. Volume 1 International Standard Book
Number: 0-88459-000-3.

Manufactured in the United States of America.
Printed and bound by the W.A. Krueger Company,
Brookfield, Wisconsin.
Color separations by Fotolithomec, Milan, Italy.

Publishers

Plenary Publications International,
Incorporated, 300 East 40th Street,
New York, 10016.

Allen Davenport Bragdon, Publisher
and Editor-in-Chief of the Family
Creative Workshop.

Nancy Jackson, Administrative Assistant.
Ronald Gross, Graphics Consultant.
Donna Lawson, Editorial Consultant.
Dick Swift, Photography Consultant.

Allen Davenport Bragdon

Walter Ian Fischman

Jacqueline Heriteau

Susan Lusk

Frank Lusk

Francesca B. Morris

Editorial Preparation

Wentworth Press, Incorporated,

Walter Ian Fischman, Director.
Jacqueline Heriteau, Editor.
Francesca B. Morris, Executive Editor.
Dorothy Chamberlain, Copy Chief.
Diana M. Walton, Associate Editor.
Donal Dinwiddie, Features Editor.
Anthony Whittier, Outdoors Editor.
William C. Mulligan, Music Editor.
Nona Remos, West Coast Crafts Editor.
Barbara Wrenn, Appalachian Crafts Editor.
M. G. Ames, New England Crafts Editor.
Katherine Varrone, Patterns Consultant.
J. D. King, Gardening Consultant.
Stuart James, Outdoors Consultant.

Design and Photography

Susan Lusk, Art Director.
Frank Lusk, Director of Photography.
Lionel Freedman, Photography Consultant.

Photographers: Eric Koniger, New York;
Stephen McCarroll, West Coast;
Paul Carpenter, Appalachia;
Susan Meiselas, New England.

Technical Illustrators: Peter Kalberkamp,
Maggie MacGowan, Clarice Borio.

Production and Traffic

Joanne McGrath, Manager; David Sachs,
Ann LeMoine, Maxine Krasnow.

For this volume

Ted Montgomery, Joe Gude,
Assistant Craftsmen, supergraphic
section, Acrylics. Jay Jonas, Editor,
American Indian Crafts, Basketry.
Thalia Larkin Erath, Assistant Editor,
historical research, Animal Dolls.

Illustrators: James Fragnito, Ant Farms,
Airplanes of Paper; Martin Trossman,
Antiquing; Peggy Wolfman, Steve LePage,
American Indian Crafts.

Technical assistance and materials for
Afghan Stitch, courtesy of Reynolds Yarns.
Appliqued quilt designs, courtesy of
The Stearns and Foster Company.
Technical assistance and materials
for telescope section of Astronomy,
courtesy of Edmunds Scientific Company.

A Word from the Editor-in-Chief

If I had only one phrase to describe what this set of books is all about, I would have to say that it is an encyclopedia of traditional and contemporary crafts. Clearly, no single phrase can encompass what goes into a practical, illustrated teaching and reference resource of this scope.

I titled this project **The Family Creative Workshop** from the germination of the idea, because I wanted it to supply readers of any age and all degrees of skill with a complete range of craft projects they could turn their hands to at any time in their lives. I envisioned it as a school-in-the-home, teaching useful and rewarding skills that people would take pride in, giving them the means of expressing their own creative imaginations. And I wanted it to be inviting and interesting to read, as well as serving as a useful, definitive reference work.

It was time, too, it seemed to me, to recapture and preserve knowledge that the parents of our grandparents had. Much of this knowledge that we now think of as crafts allowed them to survive or supplied the small comforts that now come so easily to us. These same craft skills can enrich our lives today in many different ways when we apply them to modern, man-made materials, as well as the traditional, natural ones available to our great-grandparents.

But the materials or tools we work with are not all that important. What counts most is the sure knowledge that few things work as well as our own hands. The satisfaction of making something ourselves—something lasting, something beautiful, something only we could have made—is rich and rare.

This is the idea behind the Blue Mountain Crafts Council. It was established to find skilled people who are expert in crafts and who are willing to help describe their skills in ways that make it easy for others to follow in their footsteps and develop their own variations. I have tried with these books to achieve the objectives of the Council by applying the professional techniques of contemporary illustrative publishing to this concept.

You will notice that we have interpreted the word "crafts" broadly, to include any activity that applies the discipline of a skill to achieve a desired result now or at the time the craft was developed. In fact, a few of the projects in these books are activities that require skills, but don't produce tangible objects. Some are included because the skills are in danger of being lost; some, like doing card tricks, because they are great fun; and some, like cryptography, because it is interesting to know how something is done even if we never expect to try it ourselves.

Men and women skilled in a lot of useful crafts have contributed to the creation of these books—artisans, researchers, teachers, writers, artists, photographers, designers, engravers, editors, printers, papermakers, and binders, to name a few. They applied their talents partly because they, too, liked the idea of making this kind of book, and to them, I express my appreciation.

I hope you and your family will use these books until they are dog-eared. They can take it. That's what they're for.

Allen D. Bragdon

Contents

How this encyclopedia is organized

The titles of the alphabetical entries define a craft, skill, material, or activity. Entries average ten pages in length, and each includes an introduction, followed by illustrated step-by-step instructions for making a variety of specific objects or for developing useful skills. The titles of related alphabetical entries are given at the end of each entry.

The volumes contain an average of twelve entries each. Page numbers run sequentially throughout the set. A concluding **Master Index** volume classifies all the entries and the individual projects within those entries under the following categories: **Craft and Technique; Materials;** approximate **Cost of Materials;** suggested **Age Level;** and estimated **Time** required for

The Project-Evaluation Symbols appearing in the title heading at the beginning of each project have these meanings:

Range of approximate cost:

¢ Low: Under $5, or free and found natural materials

$ Medium: About $10

$$ High: Above $15

Estimated time to completion for an unskilled adult:

⊠ Hours

🕐 Days

Weeks

Suggested level of experience:

🕴 Child alone

👫 Supervised child or family project

🕴 Unskilled adult

🕴 Specialized prior training

Tools and equipment:

Small hand tools

Large hand and household tools

Specialized or powered equipment

an unskilled adult to complete the the project.

How to select a project that matches your specific needs and interests
The **Project-Evaluation Symbols,** left, can tell you at a glance about each project, and the opposite page shows a composite, sample page and describes the many instructional and reference aids you will find in every entry.

Then look at the **Table of Contents** (on page 7 here). It tells you a great deal more about what you will find in each volume than most contents pages do. It introduces you to the experienced artisans who will personally guide you through their crafts. It tells you exactly what objects you will learn to make or what specific knowledge and skills you can acquire.

Somewhere among the entries and projects in this volume, and in every volume in this encyclopedia, we expect that anyone in your family of any age and any degree of skill will find something he or she would like to learn to do. There are in each volume: a project for your family to do together; something that is interesting just to read about; a creative activity for a child; an idea for a gift; a section you may turn to later to help you fix up something around the house.

Each entry teaches you a new skill or expands one you already have
Select almost any entry. It starts out by telling you where and when and why that craft originated. Then it illustrates and describes—much like a recipe—the materials and tools you will work with, where to find them, and what special terms mean. The first project within each alphabetical entry usually is an easy one—an introduction to the basics of the craft, where you learn how to handle the materials and become accustomed to the tools. The project may be a good rainy-day activity for a child. Or you may be able to finish it quickly and hold the result in your hands in a few hours.

Subsequent projects become more challenging and provide original

designs and ideas for taking off on your own. You are always working with real craftsmen—women or men who have been trained in that skill, usually have worked at it professionally, and frequently have taught it. They share their knowledge, help you through the tricky parts, point out shortcuts—as if you were an apprentice working with them in their shop or studio.

How the illustrations help guide you from step to step
The first large picture in each alphabetical entry usually shows how one of the projects in that entry looks when it is finished. The in-process photographs are numbered sequentially throughout each entry. The how-to drawings, diagrams, and patterns are called "figures" and are identified by letters. Figure A is the first drawing in the entry, figure B the second, and so on alphabetically to the end of that entry.

When the craftsman who is describing a procedure in the text also wants to demonstrate a sequence of steps in pictures, the text refers you to those illustrations by letter or number. These illustrations nearly always are on the same page as the text or on the page facing it.

The patterns in this encyclopedia are original designs created by the project's artist or craftsman—except for occasional historic or classic symbols and designs.

To sum it up
Life is more interesting if we know about a lot of things. We understand better and enjoy more when we can appreciate what other people have put into making something we see in their homes, what we buy in a store or see on display in a store, a museum, or a book. The simple fun of trying something new, the private satisfaction of completing something challenging, the personal pride we take in showing or giving or using something we ourselves have made—all these things open windows in our lives that too often remain closed. This set of books was made to have fun with, to help, and, hopefully, to pry open some windows.

A Guide to the Page

This composite page shows the instructional techniques and reference aids used throughout The Family Creative Workshop.

Alphabetical entry title appears at the top of most pages, as an aid to quick reference.

Craft and process category identifies each of more than 900 projects in this encyclopedia by one of the many categories in the craft field. All the projects are listed under the appropriate categories in one of the indices in the Master Index volume.

Project title pinpoints the specific object or skill each of the several projects in the entry teaches you how to make or master.

Project-evaluation symbols tell at a glance the practical things you want to know when you are looking for a project matching your needs precisely: approximate cost, time to completion, level of difficulty, type of tools.

Text provides historical background and interesting applications of the craft; describes tools, terms, materials, sources of supply; suggests craftsmen's shortcuts; simplifies otherwise complicated procedures by breaking them down into logical stages and then into easy steps.

In-process photographs record exactly how a skilled artisan accomplishes the steps of his craft, especially any difficult ones. The captions explain the steps in simple, brief terms for the beginner.

Step by step line drawings clarify techniques by showing only the essential elements of a procedure in an uncluttered sketch or diagram.

Craftnotes are inserted in appropriate entries throughout the volumes, as separate sections. They describe basic procedures, skills, tools, and materials common to many crafts.

Cross references guide you to other alphabetical entries using related materials and techniques or offering projects with similar end uses.

AMERICAN INDIAN CRAFTS

LEATHER CRAFTNOTES

The following leathers are listed in the order of their availability and are recommended for making moccasins.
Cowhide: After initial tanning, cowhide is ¼-inch thick and fairly stiff. The tanneries then split it into the desired weights of top grain and suede splits (suede on both sides). The standard unit of leather thickness is the ounce. One ounce equals 1/64 inch. After being split, leather is processed for color, flexibility and surface texture.
Vesting Leather: These moccasin tops are made of vesting leather.
Soft Bag Leather: Similar to vesting leather, but twice as heavy.
Latigo and Other Oil-tanned Leathers: I use it for all my moccasin soles. Light, strong, and moisture-resistant.
Horsehide: Excellent texture and strength, but can be hard to find.
Elk and Moose Hide: Indian materials. If available in correct weight, use it.

Leather Suppliers
Good leather is expensive, but no more so than good fabric. Cowhide costs between fifty cents and one dollar a square foot at this writing—15 to 30 square feet per half hide. Few suppliers will cut up a half hide.
  The best and most economical suppliers of high quality leather in small quantities are the jobbers of garment,

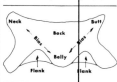

bag, and belt leathers located in the leather districts of large cities. Craftpeople and leather shops usually deal with the leather-district tradesmen. Look in the classified directory of the largest city near you, under the listing "Leather."
  Individual leather shops are geared to marketing their own products and are not always willing to sell skins. Most often they sell their scraps already packaged. These packages are something of a gamble, and often the contents are pieces too small to finish a project, or scraps of poor quality are included.

Leathercraft
Apache moccasins

When man first came to the North American continent, he probably was wearing some sort of leather footwear. In the time between that migration and the advent of white men, the original footwear patterns were adapted to divergent climates and terrains encountered by the Indian nations. Anthropologists believe that the Apache was one of the last Indian tribes to migrate south into what is now the United States, so it is not surprising that some of their high-topped-moccasin patterns resemble Eskimo mukluks—soft boots of sealskin or reindeer skin—and other northern footwear.

Some Tips for the Beginner
Three pieces are required for this Apache moccasin: Sole, vamp, and back.
  I have found that the most effective way to fit a moccasin perfectly is to make the pieces in that sequence, that is, to make the pattern for a piece only after the preceding piece has been completed. In this way, the pieces are fitted to each other, rather than being cut out all together before being assembled. I measure the vamp piece on my foot without first creating a separate pattern for it. After you have made your first pair, you may develop your own techniques.
  I have chosen to describe the making of the low-top, or short-style,

28: The top of the vamp piece should be about three inches wide. It should taper smoothly from points shown as C and D in figure N.

29: Marking side edges of the vamp prior to trimming. Note the awl-pierced front edge of the vamp piece. Line shows vamp tapering to a three-inch-wide top.

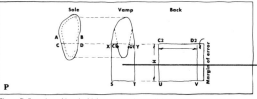

Figure P: Steps in making the high-top moccasin parallel steps for low-top version. Distance between C1, D1, measured around the heel, equals distance C2, D2.

For additional crafts and projects, see "Basketry," "Beadwork," "Belts and Buckles," "Canoeing," "Carryalls," "Flowers, Artificial," "Jewelry," "Leather Braiding," "Mineralogy," "Pottery," "Sandalmaking," "Shelters," "Silvercraft," "Survival Techniques," "Tooling," "Totem Poles," "Vegetable Dyes," "Weaving."

ACRYLICS
Plastic Versatility

Acrylics certainly fit the now generation. Hard as rock music, brilliant as a poster, and with no ties to the past, this laboratory miracle really does its own thing. Chemically speaking, acrylic materials are a sort of one-man band—they show up in so many forms. Spawned in the chemical lab, acrylic is a mixture of a liquid monomer with a powdered polymer. When these are combined into a loose muck, or slurry, and subjected to heat, one final result can be hard, flat, crystal-clear sheets like the ones used for the room-divider project shown here.

But that's not all. By a shift of chemical proportions, a similar combination can form a thick liquid, about the consistency of maple syrup, that cures into hard, crystal-clear blocks. Juggle the ingredients a bit more and you will wind up with a paint whose bold, driving colors have made it a favorite with many artists.

Material with New Potential

Acrylic materials don't really have a history, because they are so new. But there is a school of contemporary artists and craftsmen who are experimenting with far-out applications. They believe the material in its many variations is perfectly suited to the designs and projects they are creating. They like and utilize the hard-edged, pulsating colors, the pure transparency, the freedom to try new shapes and ideas not at all in the traditional idiom.

Certainly, acrylic materials open the door for new techniques and applications that are usable by novice craftsmen as well as by professionals. Much potential is built into the plastic itself. A sheet can be cut with hand tools or power equipment in straight lines or curves (see the entry "Plastics"). It can be drilled and shaped. Heated, it can be bent into gentle loops or the most intricate spirals.

Even gluing offers an opportunity for new applications. No ordinary adhesive holds the plastic sheets together. Instead, the glue is really a solvent that softens the material in a thin line until the two surfaces flow together and cure into an almost invisible joint.

Eddie Grinberg is primarily an artist. However, he is also an architect, illustrator, inventor, and craftsman. Born in France, he has worked there as well as in Israel and the United States. He has won notice for the design of a bold visual concept for subway stations in New York City, where he now lives. He also plays jazz piano.

Glass and Plastics
Room divider

Perhaps I enjoy working with acrylic sheets because I am an architect. Lines, edges, and colors are as sharp and clear as a blueprint. But the material isn't nearly as hard as the glass it resembles. It scratches easily. Housekeeping requires gentle washing with mild soap and water applied with a soft cloth, careful drying, and occasional polishing with clear paste wax. In general, handle acrylic plastic like the art object it is.

Material

I used an acrylic sheet known as Plexiglas to make the room divider here. Similar materials are sold under such trade names as Lucite and Acrylite. To keep hard work to a minimum, I always have acrylic cut and edge-polished by the supply house (for a small extra charge). Large-city phone books list such suppliers under the heading "Plastics."

Room divider on opposite page weds two forms of acrylic and serves two purposes: open, it divides a room; closed, as it appears at right, it becomes a sculptural form.

1: For this project you will need either a spray gun with paint and thinner or an assortment of aerosol spray paints in cans. Also get masking tape, razor knife, ruler, and drill, screwdriver, and hinges and screws or Mylar tape.

Although this screen was made of a ¼-inch-thick sheet of acrylic, the same material in ⅜-inch thickness would make a sturdier project. Unfortunately, this dimension is not as readily available.

The paint used is also acrylic. I like to use a spray gun for this type of painting, so I can buy basic colors and mix them to get exactly the shade I want. However, paint from aerosol spray cans will also work. Be sure to buy acrylic paint. It is usually identified as such on the label. If you have any doubts, ask questions at the paint store. Not all paints will adhere properly to an acrylic sheet.

To attach the sections of the divider, you can go one of two routes. The screen shown in the color photographs (pages 10 and 11) is held together with tiny metal hinges; plastic tape makes a stronger joint but is harder to apply. Use Mylar tape (sold in large art-supply stores) in ¾-inch or 1-inch width. For this project, you also will need standard masking tape. To protect floors, buy a paper drop cloth or save a stack of newspapers.

Tools

If you are going to follow my routine and have the plastic cut to size at the supply house, you will not need much in the way of tools. A drill and very small bits are required to attach the hinges (if you don't use tape). Although I use an electric drill, you can get by quite nicely with an egg-beater type of hand drill. Ruler, razor knife or single-edged razor blade, small print roller, and hair drier complete the list of tools.

2: Don't remove the protective paper attached to the surfaces of each acrylic sheet; instead, on it mark guidelines for the pattern. With a sharp blade, cut through paper along these lines, taking care not to gouge the soft plastic below.

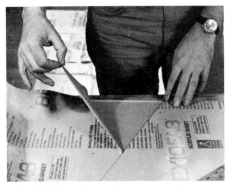

3: Peel off sections of paper covering the areas you are going to paint. It is fastened with rubber cement and comes off easily. Make sure the remaining paper is left firmly in position, to protect edges of the sprayed-on pattern.

4: Take a little extra time to mask off the edges of each sheet. This will give a more professional look to the finished project. Tear off strips of masking tape of the proper length, and press them into place along edges. Fold excess underneath.

5: Spray on the first layer of
paint, working away from the paper edge.

6: Note how the coating is softly shaded.
Do this in stages, not all at once.

7: When paint is fully dry, flip the
panel over, and spray the reverse side.

Painting Procedures Are Standard

Basic coloring technique is quite simple. The plastic panel already has
a protective paper covering on each side, and you can use this paper mask
to stencil out areas on which you don't want paint. Plan these masked-off
areas carefully. It isn't easy to re-attach the paper. Once you have
peeled it loose, it is difficult to get the edges pressed down firmly
enough to create sharp, perfectly formed color lines.

The painting procedure is the same whether you use a spray gun or a can
of spray paint. Mix paint thoroughly. Shake the spray can until agitator
ball rattles, then continue shaking one more minute. When you are ready
to paint, measure to make sure you are the proper distance from the
surface—for aerosol paints, this is usually about eight inches; for spray
guns it's sometimes a bit more. Be sure to check the spray-gun directions
or those on the label of the aerosol spray-paint can.

Common Mistakes You Can Avoid

Do not commit the common error of holding your arm still and moving the
spray gun by swinging your wrist. If you do this, you will end up with a
big paint blob in the center and thin edges. Instead, hold your wrist
steady, and paint by moving your entire arm across the surface, keeping
the gun at the same distance and angle at all times. Work in a series of
overlapping horizontal stripes as you cover the panel.

Don't try to zero in precisely on the right and left margins of the
panel. Instead, begin spraying before you come to the first edge, spray
across the sheet, and continue spraying a little past the plastic. In
this manner, you will maintain an even density of paint. Remember
that several thin coats are better than one heavy coat.

Yes, Practice Does Help

When it comes to paint, acrylics won't tolerate mistakes, because there is
no way to wipe off the coating and start over. Test color and technique
by practicing first on paper and then on scrap plastic (some colors look
fine until you hold them up to the light). Provide lots of ventilation
whether you use an aerosol can or a spray gun. Paint stores sell
inexpensive face masks that filter out airborne paint droplets. Follow
all other safety precautions on the paint-can label.

13

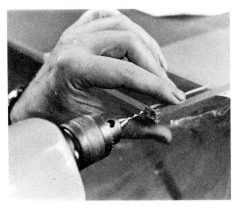

8: Drill tiny holes to fasten hinges to the edges of acrylic panels. Then carefully turn in small flat-head sheet-metal screws. Do not use force or the plastic will crack.

Joining the Panels

There are two ways to join the panels of the room divider. In the version pictured on page 10, I used little brass hinges from the hardware store. This method works, but the resulting joint is not superstrong. There is an alternate way to do the job.

Strange as it may seem, you can make a stronger hinge using plastic tape. Not just any tape will do. Be sure to buy Mylar pressure-sensitive tape in ¾-inch or 1-inch width. This will hold tenaciously to the plastic, yet you can flex it back and forth almost forever.

However, there is a definite knack to applying this tape, and until you learn how to do it, the tape is likely to show white with trapped air bubbles. See photographs 9 through 11 for how to apply it.

Designs are Unlimited

I have left the matter of paint designs for the end because I don't think it should present any problems. If that sounds like a strange statement coming from an artist-craftsman, let me explain.

My goal was to get you interested in this project—to pass along to you some of the pleasure and excitement that working with acrylics gives me. Once you have determined to sample the fun, you will probably prefer to create or adapt your own design ideas. If not, or if you would feel safer starting on firmer ground, use the design shown on page 10. It is an easy shape, with straight lines, and is so simple you don't even need a pattern.

9: Mylar tape makes a stronger hinge, but care is needed in applying it. Starting at one edge of the joint between panels, stick the tape in place. Press it down with a small rubber roller (from photography or art-supply store), to erase bubbles.

10: An ordinary hair dryer will help solve the problem if, despite your care, the tape still retains a network of air bubbles. With the dryer, warm the tape thoroughly; then use the roller once more, working toward tape edges. Cover small section at a time.

11: With panels folded together, apply a U-shape strip of tape, as shown here. For strength, tape is required on both sides of the joint. If necessary, follow up with the dryer-and-roller technique.

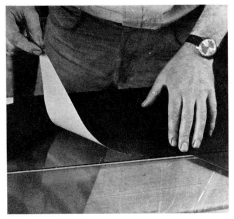

12: Peel off the last of the protective paper covering. In general, it is best to leave paper in place as long as possible, so the plastic surfaces will not become scratched during the construction.

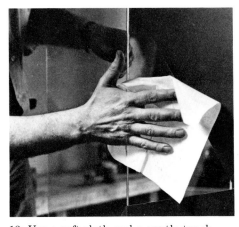

13: Use a soft cloth and a gentle touch to polish the acrylic plastic. A damp cloth will cut down on dust attraction. Paste car wax, applied in a thin layer and gently buffed, will preserve sheen.

Glass and Plastics
Poured acrylics

¢ ☒ 🚶 🛩

Funny how they accumulate, all those bits and pieces saved as reminders of good times, important times, other days, other people. There are, for example, the sea shells the kids gathered at the beach last summer. There's that Willkie button you have had forever. The big copper penny from that trip to London several years ago, or the Kennedy half dollar you've been saving. Don't forget the butterfly that is the pride of your daughter's collection. How about the ticket stubs, polished stones, brass button, locket key, bracelet charm, World War II medal, miniature doll—the list of such fragments is endless.

What are you going to do with all those things? Will souvenirs merely pile up until they burst from closets and drawers to engulf the entire household?

Fortunately, there is a craft activity that can transform these odds and ends into beautiful and charming objects. The technique is called embedment, and it is done with acrylic plastic. This material is not the same as that used to create the room divider. The name is the same and the chemical formula is similar, but the properties are vastly different.

It is just this difference that makes possible a whole new list of craft items. In this form (and combined with other plastics), acrylic modified polyester-based resin is a slow-moving liquid that pours like country molasses. When another chemical, called a catalyst, is added to it, the soft plastic turns first to a stiff jelly and then into a rock-hard substance that remains crystal clear. Because of these unique properties, you can embed in a transparent block all sorts of objects.

Although the plastic is poured in layers, one layer blends so perfectly with the next that you never will be able to discern the joint between them. This is craftwork where a small investment in patience pays dividends because the task is easy, the praise high.

Gary Zeller operates a manufacturing plant and a workshop called The Plastics Factory in New York City. He also teaches students at Pratt Institute how to work with plastics; is a craftsman, designer and consultant.

Embedments are not necessarily small. This huge memorabilia coffee table by no means represents the size limit. But it is wise to begin with smaller projects.

14: Pour embedment materials into smaller containers to ease handling. Shown here are: Front row: Catalyst in eyedropper bottle, mixing container, paste wax. Back row: Casting plastic (in cut-down detergent bottle), additive for smoother casting, and liquid mold release.

15: Many items in the kitchen make excellent and inexpensive molds. Easily identifiable above are such everyday objects as flexible ice-cube tray, muffin tin, jelly molds, a tin can, soft-plastic mixing bowls, and a ladle.

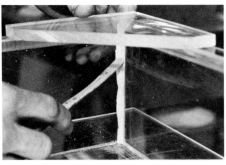

16: Apply a thin strand of rope-type window caulking (sold in hardware stores) to smooth off corners of sharp-edged molds. Smooth to a rounded cove shape.

17: Apply a coat of mold release, to make certain the hardened casting will leave the mold easily. Flow on a generous layer as it comes from the container; let dry.

18: Wipe on a coat of paste car wax after the mold release is thoroughly dry, as insurance mold will release casting. Keep the wax layer thin, and buff smooth.

19: Use a hair drier to warm the mold and dry surface, mold release, and wax. Moisture in the mold could cause white spots, and even cracking, in the casting.

Use stock materials when you try plastic embedment, and keep notes on how they work, to find the brands that produce the results you like best. Don't mix manufacturers' products; use basic plastic, catalyst, and additives made by the same company. Later you may want to try non-fracture additives, accelerators to speed hardening, and other magic chemicals. (I formulate my own plastic materials to get the exact combination I want.)

Mold Making

Rigid acrylic sheet makes a fine mold. Cut sections of the plastic, and fasten them together, using solvent-type adhesive and hollow-needle applicator (figure A1). To make certain the mold does not warp, reinforce it with wood strips underneath. Drill and countersink holes in the base (figure A2). Drive in screws until heads are flush with plastic (figure A3).

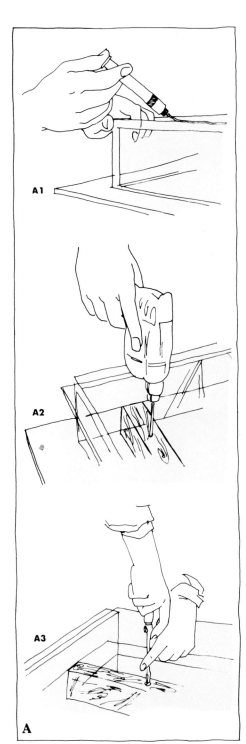

A1

A2

A3

A

16 Figure A: Assembling acrylic mold.

20: Measure the exact quantity of liquid-plastic material needed for each layer poured. Proportions are critical. Follow instructions on plastic label.

21: Only small quantities of catalyst are needed to start the hardening action. Use an eyedropper here, but do it strictly by the book or the plastic won't harden.

Add more bracing at the corners or along the sides of the mold wherever extra support may be useful, as shown in figure B. If in doubt, always overbuild. The extra work is minor when compared with the task of trimming down a lopsided or bulging embedment.

Tools

Strictly speaking, molds are not tools. However, you will need them. To start, buy polyethylene molds in a craft-supply store. These are made of soft, waxy plastic. Castings readily pop loose from them. Experiment with ice-cube trays (the soft-plastic type) for small embedments such as rock samples or insects. Glass jars can be used only once, because you have to break them (gently) to release the casting.

One small item that makes casting much easier is quite inexpensive, but you need a good supply—stirring sticks. You should have them in a series of sizes. Buy them by the box. Get coffee stirrers and tongue depressors for small jobs, paint paddles for big ones.

Measurements Are the Key

Most proportions are determined by volume: ounces or drops. For this, measuring cups and eyedroppers are fine. Later, as you get into larger work, you will probably find that it is handier to weigh the ingredients. Accuracy will demand that you use a reasonably precise scale, but a good kitchen unit will serve perfectly well unless you are planning to turn professional and open a factory.

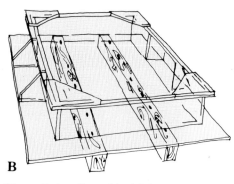

B

Figure B: Acrylic mold with bracing.

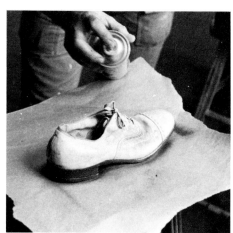

22: Some objects require special treatment before embedding. Porous materials, such as this leather shoe, must be sprayed with acrylic to seal the surface.

23: Tiny molds like the one shown here require the same base or first layer as the largest mold does. Pour the bottom layer no more than ⅛ inch thick.

24: If the object you are embedding tends to curl away from the plastic, press it down lightly. Let base layer harden to gel stage before pouring next layer.

25: Coins sometimes cause the plastic to crack as it sets. To prevent this, pour in several thin layers of plastic, letting each gel before you pour the next.

17

26: When using a large mold such as this one, make sure it is exactly level, so that the plastic will fill it in a series of thin, perfectly even layers.

27: If you try to hurry the job, bubbles may form in the plastic. To minimize the risk, pour the plastic down a stick as you feed it slowly into the mold.

28: Add objects to be embedded as soon as the bottom layer sets to a rubbery consistency. In big pourings, you may embed objects in each of several layers.

29: Pour next layer, allowing proper setting time between the pours. If you rush the process or pour too thick a layer, the plastic may crack.

30: If necessary, polish casting with buffing wheel and compound, after breaking away mold to release the casting. Unmold when plastic is barely warm to the touch.

Safety Precautions

Acrylic embedment is a reasonably safe craft activity, but don't be careless. If you are making large-scale castings and using huge amounts of liquid plastic, provide plenty of ventilation. In nice weather, work near an open window or even shift the project to a screened-in porch. If your workshop is indoors, dust carefully; then set up a fan so that it moves a constant flow of fresh air through the work area. When you are making small embedments, no special precautions are needed.

Protect Sensitive Skin

If you tend to have allergic reactions, there's a chance you may get a rash from the chemicals used in this craft. Just a few precautions will help keep you free: Wear rubber gloves when handling the liquid plastic. Be careful not to spill any of the chemicals on your skin. If you do spill a chemical, a quick wash with warm water and detergent should forestall any reaction.

Clean Work Area

Plan to do most of the casting on a sturdy table covered with several layers of newspaper. When the work surface becomes messy, you can tidy up by removing the top layer. For a different reason, it is sound policy to mop the floor and vacuum dusty surfaces before you tackle any plastic-embedment project. Particles of debris drifting around in the air can settle into the wet plastic and become a permanent part of it. Most people think this fluff adds no beauty to a project. For the same reason, develop the habit of covering the mold with a sheet of clear-plastic kitchen wrap while you are waiting for layers to harden.

Clean molds and measuring containers as soon as you have finished with them. The easiest way is to soak them in a tub of hot water with detergent. Even simpler is using disposable molds and containers.

It is important to establish a standard operating routine when you embed plastic, because the work depends on precise chemical reactions. And so here, in the form of a check list, is a step-by-step casting schedule.

□ Following instructions on the container, mix the exact quantities of casting plastic and catalyst needed for the first layer. In combination, these two will change the material from a thick liquid to a clear solid.

□ Add coloring agent and any other additives you wish.

□ Stir well. Use a sort of cutting action to mix casting plastic and catalyst. The general idea is to combine them without introducing too many air bubbles into the mixture.

□ Pour into mold to form the bottom or base layer of the plastic embedment.

□ Let set until plastic reaches the rubbery stage. Do not test it with your finger, because the fingerprint would remain and be embedded. Instead, poke it with a wooden stirring stick. The plastic is ready when it is as firm as hardened gelatin and none of it sticks to the stirrer.

□ Carefully place the objects to be embedded on the base layer.

□ Mix casting plastic and catalyst for next poured layer. Pay special attention to the instructions on the label, because the proportions of catalyst to plastic change with succeeding layers. As the stratification builds up, successive layers will absorb some heat from the lower segments, and this will make them gel more quickly. For this reason, multilayered embedments are always cast in thin layers.

□ Continue mixing, pouring, embedding, and allowing to set, according to the instructions for the plastic you are using.

Small embedments are beginning projects that allow a novice craftsman to perfect plastic-casting techniques before trying a more challenging project, such as combining paper and coins in an embedment.

31: A small casting will pop loose from the mold when the plastic has cooled. To test, rap it lightly with a stirring stick. If plastic clicks, it is ready.

32: Using a medium-grade file and a very gentle touch, smooth off rough or uneven spots that may appear on the casting despite all precautions.

Single-object cubes are generally easier to cast than the disk enclosing an assortment of stones. Metal objects often heat up too quickly and crack the plastic if it is not poured in thin layers.

33: Sand the plastic after it has been filed, to remove scratch marks. Use fine, abrasive paper placed grit side up on a flat surface. Sand lightly.

34: With a stitched flannel, buffing wheel, and plastic-buffing compound, restore surface sheen after smoothing the plastic. Begin with coarse; end with fine.

35: To make the eerie hand shown here, suspend a rubber glove by the cuff, and fill with layers of plastic and marbles. Such oddball projects make their own rules, and you have to play them by ear.

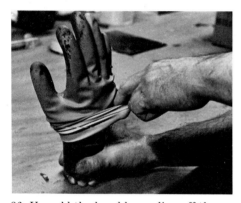

36: Unmold the hand by peeling off the rubber glove when the plastic has set and the glove feels cool to the touch. The glove can be used again if you want to cast another of these weird hands.

Although the tools and materials required for plastic embedding are quite simple, it is important to take care of them if you want to use them for future projects. Treatment of molds is critical. Do not use steel wool, scouring powder, or any similar type of harsh abrasive on them. Once you have destroyed its smooth surface, you will never again get a smooth casting from a mold. This warning applies especially to soft-polyethylene molds, as these can be abraded with your fingernail. If they become scratched, toss them out and buy new ones.

After a while, you may find that your embedment work seems to center around a few basic sizes or shapes of mold. Since molds are sometimes destroyed when they are being loosened from the casting, you may wish to build some heavy-duty, reusable ones. Make square-sided molds from wood with a hard-finish plastic-laminate bonded to the inner surfaces. The material used for counter tops is perfect for this job. Design the molds in breakaway form, so that you can remove the screws or other fasteners holding them together and can separate the sections. Used with mold release plus a well-buffed coating of paste wax, molds of this type encourage high-quality work and can be used again and again for years.

Don't Embed Everything

It is easy to be carried away by this craft activity because it produces such interesting objects. But keep this fact in mind: not everything can be embedded. The basic list of objects that cannot be successfully embedded in plastic includes anything that contains water or is too close to being alive—undried flowers, fresh bugs, and fish, for instance.

For impact, it's hard to beat the shock value of this pop-art project. Simple to make, the unusual item would be a fine gift for a member of the teen-age set.

Paint and Color
The Beetle project

"The paint brush is as mighty as the pen," claimed an anonymous graphic artist, and who is to say he may not be right? The rainbow-colored VW bug on the following pages testifies to the merits of ordinary, household, interior/exterior, acrylic enamel; imagination and energy translated into a durable, free-spirited craft object.

The colors we used,—red, orange, yellow, green, blue, and violet—are a traffic-stopper, and the design also camouflaged the dents and weathered paint, creating a new virtue from an old necessity.

Materials
Two pint cans in each color were plenty for our VW. The paint to ask for is interior/exterior acrylic enamel sold for ordinary household use, at paint, hardware, and department stores. These modern acrylic paints can be applied with a brush; they flow on smoothly; they dry quickly to a hard bright finish; and they hold up under adverse conditions. The directions that follow will be for brushed-on paint, which is cheaper and a lot easier than aerosol or machine spraying. Follow directions and recommendations on the labels carefully.

You will also need: masking tape ½-inch or ⅜-inch wide; cloth-backed emery

Joe Gude and Ted Montgomery—who designed this creative, low-cost solution to a friend's dowdy, dented VW problem— graduated together from the architecture department of the University of Cincinnati. They constructed the Lear residence, located in the mountains of Vermont, including building and designing the furniture, lighting, graphics, and general gadgetry of living. Currently, they both are freelancing in furniture design, photography, and communication arts.

37: With tape, outline color patterns. Don't get uptight about the proper spacing. It's impossible to do it wrong. With so much color, errors look intentional.

38: The first color is being applied. You will be pleased at how easily the paint flows on, and at how smooth the finished surface appears.

39: As this is an exercise in free form, you have the opportunity to reposition the tape or pull it loose and start all over if the result doesn't please you.

paper in fine and very fine grades; car wax remover; acrylic paint thinner, two, high-quality bristle brushes 3 inches and 1 inch wide; a small, pointed, touch-up brush available in most hardware stores; several rags, and a jar to hold paint thinner when you clean brushes.

Preparing the Surface
The ideal place for painting is a garage with the door open for ventilation. A shady spot outdoors will do, if you choose one away from dust, insects, and falling leaves. Avoid direct sunlight, or painting when the air temperature is below 60 degrees Fahrenheit. Prepare the car surface carefully to insure a long-lasting paint job. Then before the painting begins, remove all dirt, tar, bugs, and wax from old finish. Next, using the emery cloth, sand the surface lightly to remove the gloss of the old paint and any rust spots. Smooth the old paint carefully in areas where it is cracked, peeling, or flaking. The better this sanding job is done the better the acrylics paint will adhere. Use auto-body putty to fill in small dents and holes, but remember that people's attention will go first to the new colors, not to a few minor dents. Wipe the whole car to remove any fine particles of paint and grit. Use rags soaked in paint thinner and keep folding them to expose a fresh surface. When you can run your finger over the surface of the car and pick up no dust, you are ready to tape and paint.

Decorating the Car

With a piece of chalk or a marking pen, roughly indicate your painting design, getting an approximate idea of the areas for each color. Apply tape over the sketched lines by using the thumb of one hand to press the tape onto the

40: Tape outlines of areas you will paint.

Problem

41: The color is being applied.

42: Beginnings of the rainbow effect.

car body, the other hand to hold the unwinding roll. With practice, you can make the tape curve where you want it. When you remove the tape after painting you will have a narrow, hard-edged strip in the original color of the car neatly separating the new acrylic colors on either side. The paint should need no thinning as it comes from the can. Begin brushing with small strokes, working from an unpainted area onto the fresh paint of your last stroke. A thin coat of paint will adhere better than a thick one and

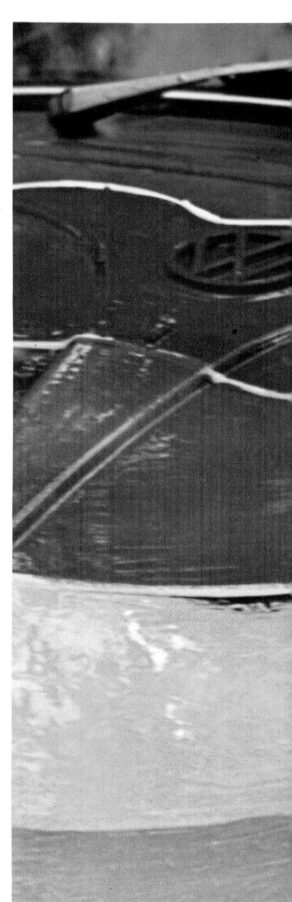

is less likely to sag or drip. A second coat is recommended, but may not be necessary to hide blemishes to your satisfaction. Follow directions on the label faithfully for drying time between coats. Within a few hours after painting, pull off the tape; the longer you leave it on the harder it is to remove without tearing. The paint doesn't need to be bone-dry before the tape is removed, only set enough not to drip or sag. As soon as the tape is off, before the paint is thoroughly dry, touch up any problem areas. Paint thinner on a rag will usually remove runs, smears, and unwanted spots and spatters at this stage. Acrylic enamels usually dry to the touch overnight, but they need as long as a month to dry thoroughly. A clear acrylic sealer may

Solution

be sprayed on top of the paint after it has had 48 hours or so to dry. But ask the advice of the local dealer and test a small area first as different paints have different characteristics. Finally, after a month of curing, you can wax the car. Test the paint first with a little wax to be sure it is cured completely. Wax may lift the paint slightly; if so, let the paint cure longer.

For related projects and crafts, see "Casting," "Mobiles," "Molds," "Pin Stripping," "Super graphics."

AFGHAN STITCH

A Crochet Favorite

Sandra Vogt, who made the granny afghan, vest, and child's skirt shown in this feature, came to crafts via the related paths of art and photography. Like many mothers, she has found that a variety of crafts can provide a creative outlet. In addition to crochet, Sandy does macrame, knitting, and sewing. The afghan on the opposite page was designed for The Family Creative Workshop by the staff of Reynolds Yarns.

The afghan stitch is a variation of crocheting based on the chain stitch. Just why it is called afghan stitch, nobody seems to know. It is sometimes called Tunisian crochet. Crochet in general is thought to have originated among the nomad tribes of Africa and Asia, which these names would seem to bear out. How the afghan (the throw or coverlet) and the stitch are related is also not clear. The Oxford English Dictionary assures us the term is not derived from Afghanistan. Perhaps it can be assumed the stitch came first and the coverlets made with the stitch got their names that way. Certainly it is a nice, thick, warm stitch ideal for a cozy throw. The even firmness of the finished stitch has, in recent years, made it popular as a background for colorful cross-stitch embroidery.

Needlecrafts
Vest and child's skirt

The Vest

A handsome, first venture to test your skill with afghan stitch is the vest shown on page 26. For key to abbreviations, see page 30.

Sizes: Directions are for misses' size 8. Changes for sizes 10 and 12 are in parentheses.

Materials: 2 (3-3) 4-oz. skeins Yellow Knitting Worsted. A few strands of Blue Worsted. Afghan hook size 7. Steel crochet hook size E. Yarn needle with large eye.

Gauge: 9 stitches = 2 inches; 3 rows = 1 inch.

Back: Ch 73 (77-81). Work in afghan st for 10 inches, or desired length to underarm. **Shape Armhole:** Dec by sl st across next 4 sts. Work across row in pattern to last 4 sts, and sl st these. Fasten and cut yarn. Rejoin yarn to continue return row. Dec 2 sts at each end of next 3 (3-4) rows. Work in pattern until armhole is 7½ inches (7½ inches-8

inches). **Shape Shoulder:** Ch 1, sc across. Turn, ch 1, sl st across 8 sts, sc across to last 8 sts, sl st. Fasten.

Left Front: Ch 37 (39-41). Work in pattern until same length as back to underarm. **Shape Armhole:** Work as Back. At same time, dec 2 sts at neck edge every 4th row until 16 sts remain. Work until armhole measures same as Back, ending at neck edge. **Shape Shoulder:** Work same as shoulder on Back.

Right Front: Work same as Left Front, reversing all shaping.

Finishing: Weave shoulder and side seams. Block or steam-press. Work 1 row sc around entire vest and armholes. Work 1 row of cross-stitch around front and neck edges.

These old-fashioned patchwork squares, worked in a variety of crochet stitches, are often referred to as afghan stitch. This type of patchwork is correctly called Granny Squares. The throw on the opposite page has been worked in true afghan stitch, which produces a firm, warm, evenly textured surface. To make afghans like the one above, see the "Granny Squares" entry in a later volume.

This afghan looks like a traditional Aran knit, but actually it is crocheted in panels of afghan stitch. Directions for making it are on page 29.

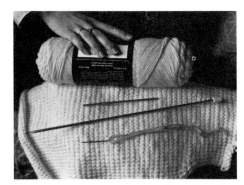

1: The basic materials you will need to do the afghan-stitch project: yarn, a crochet hook, an afghan hook, and sometimes a yarn needle.

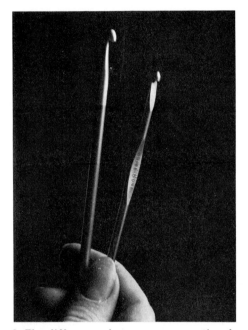

2: The differences between a conventional crochet hook and an afghan hook shown here. The crochet hook is much shorter and has a flattened area so it can be grasped comfortably. The afghan hook is longer and smooth. This is because, in afghan stitch, an entire row is held on the hook. In crochet, only a few loops are kept on.

3: Close-up of the detail of the edging on the vest, showing the cross-stitch embroidery on both right and wrong sides.

Afghan stitch is ideal for making warm outerwear with a tailored look. Sandra designed and made this vest to wear during the chill of early spring planting season.

Child's skirt

This charming little-girl's skirt has a tweedy pink-and-white texture because the rows were worked in alternating colors.

Sizes: Directions are for size 4. Changes for sizes 6 and 8 are in parentheses.

Materials: One 4-oz. skein White Knitting Worsted; 1 4-oz. skein Pink. Afghan hook size 7. Steel crochet hook size 5. One yard 1-inch elastic.

Gauge: 5 stitches=1 inch; 3 rows=1 inch.

Pattern Stitch: Row 1: Work 1st half in Pink; work return half in White. Row 2: Work 1st half in White; work return half in Pink.

Skirt Back: Begin at lower edge with Pink, and chain 65 (69-73). Work in afghan stitch and color pattern for 2 inches (3-4 inches) from start, or 9 inches less than desired skirt length. Dec 1 st at each end of new row. Repeat dec every 2 inches 3 times

Tweedy effect is given to skirt executed in plain afghan stitch by using a combination of wool colors. Sandra designed skirt for her young neighbor, Darlene.

4: Detail of waistband casing that holds the elastic in place inside the skirt. Instructions for casing and inserting elastic are in directions at left.

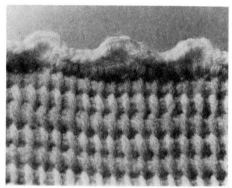

5: Close-up of the skirt edging, showing scalloped picot trim that is crocheted around skirt bottom. Instructions for edging are given under Finishing, at left.

6: Afghan stitch in the making. Note how the afghan hook passes under the vertical bar of the previous row to pull up a loop.

more. Work even until piece measures 11 inches (12-13 inches), or ½ inch shorter than desired skirt length. Sc across top. Fasten and cut yarn. Pick up White, and sc across previous sc row. Fasten and cut yarn.

Front: Work same as for Back.

Finishing: Steam-press pieces, or block. Backstitch or weave side seams. With White, work bottom edging: 2 sc, * (1 hdc, 2 dc, 1 hdc) in next st, 4 sc. * Repeat from * to * all around bottom. Fasten and cut yarn.

Casing: With White, join yarn to inside top edge, * make a chain 1 inch long, sl st in stitch ½ inch to left in row 1 inch below, make a ch 1 inch long, sl st at top of skirt ½ inch to left of last st. Repeat from * around top of skirt. Cut elastic to waist measurement. Weave elastic through casing; sew ends together. See photograph 4.

Afghan stitch, with its smooth surface and stable edges, makes this trim game-room pillow that doubles as a tic-tac-toe board. X and O markers are movable.

Needlecrafts
Tic-tac-toe pillow

Directions to make pillow and markers:
Size: Approximately 14 inches square.

Materials: 4-ply acrylic-and-nylon Knitting Worsted, 1 skein each of White, Black, and Red. Afghan hook size H, 14 inches long. Crochet hook size F for markers. Yarn needle. Pillow form. Coffee-stirrer sticks cut into ten 2¼-inch lengths.

Gauge: Afghan stitch:17 stitches = 4 inches; 7 rows = 2 inches. Finished square = 3¾ inches. Markers: 5 sc = 1 inch.

Board Squares: Make 9 White and 9 Black. Ch 14. Pull up a loop in 2nd ch from hook and in each ch across (14 loops on hook). Yo, and draw yarn through first loop on hook. *Yo, and pull through 2 loops. Repeat from * across row until 1 loop remains. Work 9 more rows in afghan pattern. **Border Row:** Insert hook into center of next bar between front and back strands; yo, draw up a loop, and sc. Repeat in every bar. Work 2 sc in ch at end of row. Work 1 row of sc on side edge, inserting hook under both sides of sts. Work

3 sc in corner st, work 1 row sc on back side of bottom ch, 3 sc in corner and 1 row up side edge. End with 1 sc in top st, sl st. Fasten.

Red-Stripe Panels (2¼ inches wide finished): Make 2 panels 14 inches long and 2 panels 11 inches. Ch 8, and work in afghan pattern until correct length. There will be approximately 50 rows in the longer panels and 36 in the shorter. Work border row as in squares.

Finishing: Sl st pieces together from wrong side, inserting hook through top loops only on each side. After squares are assembled, join shorter panels to opposite sides, then longer ones. With right sides together, sl st around 3 sides. Turn to right side; insert pillow form, and whipstitch open side closed.

Markers, X: Make 10 halves. With Red and size-F crochet hook, ch 10. **Rnd 1:** Sc in 3rd ch from hook, sc in each of next 6 ch, 2 sc in last ch; working on opposite of starting-ch, 2 sc in first ch, sc in 6 ch, 2 sc in last ch. Join with sl st in ch at

beg of round. **Rnd 2:** Ch 1. Sc in first sc, sc in each of 7 sc, 2 sc in each of next 2 sc, sc in next 8 sc, 2 sc in last sc. Join in first ch-1. Break yarn, leaving 10-inch end for sewing. Fold strip in half lengthwise; insert stick; sew edges together through all loops of sc. Sew 2 together to form X shape.

Markers, O: Make 5. With Red and size-F crochet hook, ch 10. Join with sl st in first ch, to form ring. Ch 1. **Rnd 1:** 12 sc in ring. **Rnd 2:** Ch 1. Work 16 hdc in ring, covering sc of last rnd. Join in first sc. End off.

Tassels: Make 4. For each tassel, wind yarn loosely around a piece of cardboard 7 inches wide. Wind 7 times. Cut one end. Fold strands, and tie tightly about ½ inch from fold. With a yarn needle, thread yarn through tassel top, and sew loops to pillow corners. Trim evenly.

If you'd like to make a chess afghan to match the pillow, write for Kit No. 24, International Creations, Box 55, Great Neck, N.Y. 11023.

Needlecrafts
Popcorn-and-leaf afghan

The afghan shown in the color photograph on page 24 is an unusual combination of popcorns and raised leaves worked against the even, basketlike weave of plain afghan stitch. It is made in strips.

Size: Approximately 47 by 60 inches, including borders. Afghan consists of 9 Leaf Strips and 4 Popcorn Strips.

Materials: 16 4-ounce skeins Knitting Worsted, or acrylic and nylon (4-ply cream). Afghan hook size G, or use size to obtain specified gauge. Steel crochet hook size 0, for joining and borders.

Gauge: Afghan stitch: 11 stitches = 2 inches; 8 rows = 2 inches.

Note: Each Leaf Strip is 1⅝ inches wide, approximately 58¾ inches long. Each Popcorn Strip is 6 inches wide, approximately 58 inches long.

Leaf-Pattern Strip: Make 9. With afghan hook, ch 9 and work 6 rows in plain afghan st (see page 31).

Start Leaf Pattern: Row 7: Draw up a loop in 2nd, 3rd, 4th, and 5th vertical bars (5 loops on hook), make leaf as follows: Yo and draw up a loop in 3rd vertical bar from right end of strip but 3 rows below, (which is plain row 4), * yo and draw through 1 loop, yo and draw through 2 loops, yo and draw through 1 loop * (this forms a long stitch, and there will now be 6 loops on hook); yo and draw up a loop in 4th vertical bar from right end of strip, but 4 rows below, (which is plain row 3), and repeat from * to * (7 loops on hook), yo hook twice, draw up a loop in 5th vertical bar (center) from right end of strip but 5 rows below, (which is plain row 2), yo and through 1 loop, yo and through 2 loops twice, yo and through 1 loop (8 loops on hook); yo and draw up a loop in 6th vertical bar from right end of strip but 4 rows below, (which is plain row 3), and repeat from * to * (9 loops on hook); yo and draw up a loop in 7th vertical bar from right end of strip but 3 rows below, (which is plain row 4), and repeat from * to * (10 loops on hook); yo and draw through 6 loops on hook and ch 1 to close leaf; draw up a loop in each of the last 4 vertical bars in plain Row 6 (9 loops on hook). Work off as for plain afghan

st. **Rows 8 through 13:** Work in plain afghan st. Repeat Rows 7 through 13 for Leaf Pattern, or until there are 34 patterns from start, ending with pattern Row 7—238 rows worked. Bind off. (To bind off, see Craftnotes, page 30.)

Popcorn Strip: Make 4. With afghan hook ch 33 and work Row 1 and first half of Row 2 in plain afghan st. Yo and through first loop, * yo and through 2 loops twice, ch 3 (for popcorn) *, repeat from * to * 6 times more (7 popcorns); yo and through 2 loops 3 times, ch 3, repeat from * to * 6 times more, ending with yo and through 2 loops 3 times. **Row 3 and all Odd Rows:** Work plain afghan st, keep popcorns on right side. (33 loops). **Row 4:** Repeat first half of Row 2 in plain afghan st. Yo and through first loop, * yo and through 2 loops twice, ch 3 *, repeat from * to * 5 times more (6 popcorns), yo and through 2 loops 7 times, ch 3 and repeat from * to * 5 times, ending yo and through 2 loops 3 times. **Row 6:** Work first half of row 2 in plain afghan st. Yo and through first loop, * yo and through 2 loops twice *, ch 3, repeat from * to * 4 times more, yo and through 2 loops 11 times, ch 3, repeat from * to * 4 times, ending yo and through 2 loops 3 times. Continue to work 1 popcorn st fewer at each side of center plain sts. and work 4 more plain afghan sts in center on second half of every even row until there is 1 popcorn at each side and there are 27 plain sts in center (14 rows). This is the center of one diamond. Continue as before, working one more popcorn st at each side of center plain sts and 4 sts fewer in plain afghan st at center on second half of every even row until there are 14 popcorns across row. Work 1 row of plain afghan st. Work a second row of 14 popcorns for start of second diamond. Continue as before, working 1 popcorn fewer at each side, as in first diamond, until there is 1 popcorn at each side. Continue in this manner until there are 9 diamond patterns from start—

235 rows worked. Bind off.

To Join Panels: Attach yarn in first row of a diamond strip at right-hand edge. With steel crochet hook, work a sc in first row, * ch 5, skip 1 row, sc in next row at side, repeat from * to top of strip, ending 1 sc in last row. Ch 5, pick up Leaf-Pattern Strip, and work a sc in the last row of this strip. ** Ch 2, work a sl st in 3rd ch of last "loop" of Popcorn Strip, ch 2, skip 1 row of Leaf Strip, sc in next row of Leaf Strip, repeat from ** down, easing in the extra 3 rows on Leaf Strip to fit Popcorn Strip ending sc in first row of Leaf Strip. Cut yarn, and fasten. Continue to join strips in this manner, joining 2 more Leaf Strips, then 1 Popcorn Strip, 3 Leaf Strips, 1 Popcorn Strip, 3 Leaf Strips, and 1 Popcorn Strip. With steel crochet hook work 1 row of sc at each long side edge of afghan.

Borders for Each End of Afghan: Attach yarn in first row at lower edge of afghan. Ch 5, * skip 1 st, ch 5, repeat from * across lower edge of afghan, working a sc at each side of joinings with a ch 5 between. **Row 2:** Ch 3, turn * sl st in center of ch 5, ch 5, repeat from * across, ending sl st in center of ch 5. Repeat Row 2 for 2 more rows. Cut yarn and fasten.

Fringe: Cut yarn into 20-inch lengths. Attach fringe as follows: Fold 6 strands in half, and knot in first ch-5 loop. Then knot in every other ch-5 loop across lower edge. **Row 1:** Divide "tassels" in half. Skip first half of outside tassel; * knot next 2 adjoining halves together about 1½ inches from border. Repeat from * across, skipping last half-tassel. **Row 2:** Starting with free half of first tassel, knot this half together with half of second tassel, about 1½ inches down from last knot; * knot next 2 adjoining halves. Repeat from * across. Trim ends evenly.

For related projects and crafts, see "Applique," "Granny Squares," "Knitting," "Quilting," "Patchwork."

CROCHET

Abbreviations

ch	chain	rnd	round
dec	decrease	sc	single crochet
dc	double crochet	sl st	slip stitch
hdc	half double crochet	st(s)	stitch(es)
inc	increase	tr	treble crochet
*	repeat from	yo	yarn over

To Increase with Afghan Stitch: At the beginning of a row, pull up a loop in the 2nd vertical bar; then insert hook under stitch between vertical bar just worked and next one. One extra loop has been added. At end of row, make the increase loop between 2nd and 3rd vertical bars from the end.

To Decrease with Afghan Stitch: At the beginning of a row, slip hook under 2nd and 3rd upright bars, and draw up one loop. At the end of row, decrease in same manner on 2nd and 3rd bars from end.

To Bind Off: Work a single crochet in each stitch.

Single crochet

On a foundation chain, insert the hook into the second chain from the hook.

Yarn over, and draw through stitch (2 loops on hook).

Yarn over, and draw yarn through both loops.

Chain stitch

Make a slipknot, and slide on a crochet hook.

Hold crochet hook with right index finger and thumb (left if you're left-handed). Wrap yarn through fingers of other hand to provide tension, and guide with index finger.
Bring yarn over and around crochet hook.

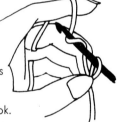

Catch yarn on hook, and pull through existing loop. Original loop slips off. Repeat for a foundation chain.

Half double crochet

Yarn over, and insert hook into third chain from hook.

Pull up a loop (3 loops on hook).

Yarn over, and draw through all 3 loops.

Slip stitch

Working on a foundation chain, skip one stitch, and insert hook in top strand of the second chain. Yarn over, and draw through both loops on hook.

CRAFTNOTES

Double crochet
Yarn over, and insert hook in fourth chain from hook.

Draw up loop (3 loops on hook).
Yarn over; pull through 2 loops.

Two loops remaining on hook.

Yarn over, and pull through last 2 loops.

Treble crochet
Yarn over twice; insert hook in fifth chain from hook.

Draw up a loop (4 loops on hook).

Yarn over; draw through 2 loops (3 loops on hook).

Yarn over; draw through 2 loops (2 loops on hook).

Yarn over; pull through last 2 loops (no loops left).

Fastening Yarn: Bring end through loop of last stitch, and cut yarn 3 or 4 inches long. Thread end on yarn needle, and weave along a row of stitches on the wrong side for a few inches. Clip excess yarn.

Blocking: On an ironing board, pin each piece of work wrong side up and to accurate measurements. Use rustproof pins. Set iron for wool, and cover work with damp cloth. Do not rest weight of iron on crocheted article, but pass iron slowly over it. Let article dry before unpinning.

Afghan stitch.
Make a chain the desired length, not including loop on hook, which counts as first stitch of next row. Insert hook in second chain, and draw up a loop.

Pull up a loop in each chain, keeping all loops on hook. (This is first half of row.)

Yarn over hook, and draw through first loop.

Yarn over hook, and draw through 2 loops. Repeat with all loops on hook. (This is second half of row.)

Remaining loop is first stitch of next row.

Insert hook in second vertical bar, and draw up a loop. Proceed across row, drawing up a loop in each vertical bar and retaining them all on hook. In last stitch, insert hook through double loop, and pull up a loop.

Return as in steps 3 and 4.

AIRPLANES OF PAPER
Glider Aerodynamics

It may be difficult to believe, but the easiest way to learn about flying is to make paper airplanes. The fundamentals of gliding flight will begin to manifest themselves as you construct, launch, and modify a paper fleet. All you need to become a paper-airplane pilot are some inexpensive supplies you most likely already have on hand.

The paper is the most important ingredient. Unless otherwise directed, use ordinary 8½-by-11-inch typing or bond paper, which is neither too stiff nor too thin. I have used paper with a light-gray or tan tint on one side for the instructional photographs of most of the planes shown here. This permits you to see more clearly exactly how and in what sequence the folds are made. Of course, you can use paper of any color—even the Sunday comics—provided it is of suitable weight. Once you get started, you will want to try different papers to see how they change a plane's flying characteristics as well as its appearance.

Don't be disappointed if your first model makes a beeline for the ground on its initial flight. This can happen. Sometimes two planes, folded the same way and made of the same paper, have totally different flight patterns. Putting a little more bend on the wings or a little more weight on the tail or simply changing a curve or a fold can have a marked effect on the way a plane flies. As you practice by making the planes described below, you will learn several of the many ways a plane's flying characteristics can be altered. Don't be afraid to experiment. Become an inventor, and design your own planes. With a little experience, you will be as good as any other paper-airplane engineer. And if you lose a bit of self-esteem when one design fails, it will return when the next one stays aloft longer than you expected it to.

Captain Ralph S. Barnaby, U.S.N.(Ret.), built and pilots his own glider, knew Orville Wright, and is a well-known air pioneer. His original paper-airplane design, the Barnaby, won a first prize in a Scientific American *contest.*

Paper Folding and Cutting
The Dartmouth Dart

A good plane to begin with is the Dartmouth Dart. According to rumor, it originated in the institution of higher learning for which it is named. A professor of economics launched the plane to demonstrate for his class a basic principle of investing in stocks: What goes up usually comes down. This is ably demonstrated by the Dart.

Few ships are as responsive in flight. To solo, grasp the fuselage from below with your forefinger and thumb, just slightly in front of the plane's midpoint. Hold the plane at shoulder height, and launch it with a slight downward thrust. The plane will probably have a brisk flight, making a graceful, looping turn before coming to rest. If it goes into a nose dive, bend up the rear of the wings slightly. You will discover that a slight bend on either wing will have a considerable effect on the plane's flight pattern. It is surprising how a little pinch here or there affects this pattern. Try making several Darts, using the same paper, but modifying the wings and stabilizers (control surfaces) in various ways. Note the difference in flying characteristics when you fold up the right wing's rear edge or bend one stabilizer a little. Also try putting an upward curve along a wing edge by rolling the paper around a pencil.

Dartmouth Dart coming in for a graceful landing. Because the Dart is easy to make, it is a good choice for your first try at folding a paper flying machine.

A

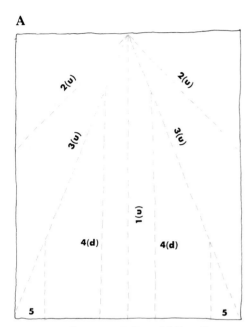

Figure A: Dartmouth Dart folding diagram. Note that (u) means fold upward at the line and (d) means fold downward.

Although the Dart uses a straightforward, gimmick-free design, there's versatility built right into the craft. It's easy to vary flight with simple bends or changes.

Try a fold down here or there. Try lighter or heavier papers. The Dart is a good plane to practice on. You should be able to create several variations on this one simple design. If you keep notes on the effects of the changes you make, you will have a useful reference for subsequent plane-designing efforts.

1: Fold a sheet of typing paper in half lengthwise 1(u), making a sharp crease. Unfold, and crease lines 2(u), figure A, so paper edges meet at center crease.

2: Fold lines 3(u) so paper edges meet the center line. Refold the center crease. Fold one 4(d) line to form a wing, as shown here. Turn plane over, and fold other 4(d).

3: Fold lines 5 to make the stabilizers, as shown here (up or down fold will work equally well). Staple or clip fuselage about a third of the way back from nose.

The plane's solid, reliable flying characteristics reflect its straightforward construction technique. Before starting work, study figure A, indicating the folding lines. None of the folding steps is at all complex, but it is important that you pay careful attention to each instruction. For example, one stage calls for you to fold the paper, crease it firmly, and then open it again before making the next fold. First creases form the fuselage or backbone of the plane. Succeeding folds make the wings, and the final paperwork takes care of the stabilizers. Staples or paper clips hold folds in position and also add flying ballast. For step-by-step directions, follow numbered photographs.

The Barnaby, an original design by Captain Ralph S. Barnaby, won the Aerobatics Professional Prize in the First International Paper Airplane Competition.

B

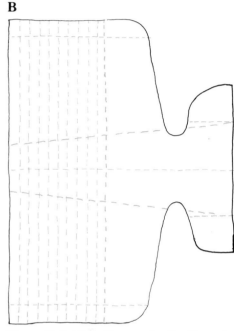

Figure B: Folding diagram for the Barnaby. Broken lines are fold lines, and solid lines are cut lines.

Paper Folding and Cutting
The Barnaby

This simply designed plane is an acrobat, or aerobat, as flying buffs call such a plane. It will perform glides, left turns, right turns, or actually come back to you—all in response to minor adjustments you can make in its wing tips or tail fins. Figure B shows the fold lines for constructing this prizewinning plane. The build-up of folds along the front edge of the wings adds weight for flying quality. Fine tuning is accomplished by gently bending the wing tips up and the tail fins down. To alter the Barnaby's flight characteristics, experiment with narrower or wider folds for wings and tail. Grasp the tail, and launch with a gentle upward thrust.

4: Fold 8½-by-11-inch paper in half, crosswise, first. Unfold, and make a series of nine ¼-inch folds lengthwise, using half the sheet. Broken lines, figure B, indicate folds.

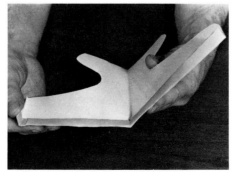

5: Fold again along the original crease, and press it firmly. Cut along solid line, as shown in figure B. Turn wing tips up, as shown here, and tail fins down. Pinch center crease at front edge and tail.

The Flying Tiger has a flatter glide than the Dart and is more stable in flight. Its shorter keel and broader wings make the difference.

Paper Folding and Cutting
The Flying Tiger

Versatility is the word for this wide-wing design. The craft is suitable for almost any experimental flying program you might want to attempt. The Flying Tiger is best constructed of heavyweight paper such as 20-pound-bond typing paper or the coated pages from a slick magazine. These provide the stiffness that makes for good flying and will permit adjustments that hold. Adjustments to wings and elevons will be easier if you don't press your original folds into razor-sharp creases.

There are several ways to improve flight stability and to vary flying characteristics. If the plane zooms up, stalls, and then flutters to earth, add another paper clip to the nose. If it heads for the ground immediately, reduce the nose weight. Adjust the elevons (the tabs marked 6 in figure C) to make changes in the flight pattern. To make the plane bank and swerve to right or left, have one elevon flat or downward

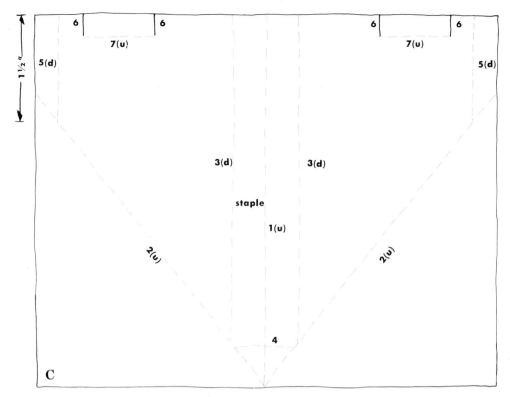

C

1½"

6   6   6   6
7(u)   7(u)
5(d)   5(d)
3(d)   3(d)
staple
1(u)
2(u)   2(u)
4

◄Figure C: Diagram and pattern. Note that (u) means fold upward on line, (d) means fold downward. Solid line means cut.

6: Crease sheet in half crosswise, 1(u). Unfold; then fold line 2(u), starting one and a half inches back and allowing the corners to overlap the center line evenly.

7: Refold along the center line to crease overlaps; then fold down the wing surfaces, 3(d), to form keel of ship. Add staple midway along keel to hold folds together.

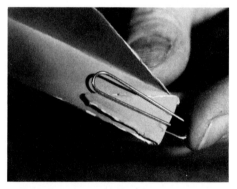

8: Fold down wing tips, 5(d), and form the elevons by cutting lines 6 and folding up the tabs at 45-degree angles, 7(u). Fold back the nose, 4, and add a paper clip.

and the other up at an angle. To lengthen gliding time (flatten glide path), try bending both upward at a steep angle. Don't be timid about changing the wing angles to various V-shapings—or even flat across. For the most part, these adjustments will affect the stability of the ship. You will quickly discover by trial and error the degree of stability you can tolerate in return for friskier performance. Generally, the deeper the V-shape of the wings, the more stable the flight attitude and the less depth needed in the keel.

Launching techniques also affect flight. Forceful thrusting upward, either level or tilted to the side, will give the longest flights, provided you have put on enough nose weight. Floating the plane into the air at low velocity and level attitude will allow it to assume its natural flight pattern immediately. Hard downward launchings with elevons bent up steeply will generally produce a moderate climb with swerve to right or left. For more unpredictable flight patterns, try launching the Flying Tiger into a gentle breeze, or whisk it straight up.

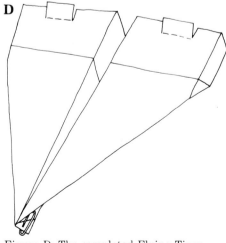

D

Figure D: The completed Flying Tiger.

▶ Figure E: Falcon folding diagram. Note that (u) means fold upward on the line and (d) means fold downward.

E

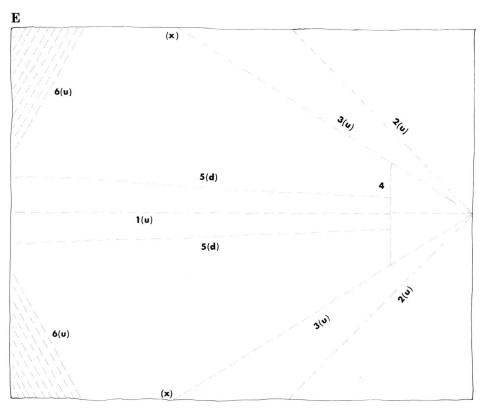

9: Fold sheet in half lengthwise, 1(u). Unfold, and crease lines 2(u) so top edges meet centerline. Fold lines 3(u) as shown. Points (x) are 4 inches from tail.

10: Refold along the centerline, 1(u). Fold back two inches of the nose tip, 4. Fold the keel line of the plane, 5(d), and put a clip in the nose, as shown here.

11: Feather, or bend up, the trailing edges of the wings, 6(u), by scoring them with a thumbnail, the scores running horizontally, vertically, or diagonally.

Paper Folding and Cutting
The Falcon

The Falcon—made from 8½-by-11-inch typing paper—is a cross between the Dart and the Flying Tiger and is more maneuverable than either. Part of the reason for this is its lack of stabilizing fins on the wings; part is the blunt, comparatively heavy nose, which tends to decrease speed, making the ship more susceptible to other influences.

Making the Falcon
Heavy paper is best for this plane. Try vellum, 20-pound bond, or a slick (coated stock) magazine cover. This weight, and the blunt nose, coupled with the trim lines, will make a speedy flyer. The Falcon can be adjusted to swerve or stall, then recover in a smooth glide. Try several launching angles, including straight up and sideways, to gain a working knowledge of its flight potential.

The secret of this model's steady course is the extra fold in the top of each wing, which provides increased airfoil effect (lift). To investigate this lift, drop the plane, nose down, from a height of ten feet or more, noting recovery. Now make an identical model from paper of half the weight, and repeat this launch; recovery will be a bit faster but time-in-air about the same. This lift also will allow the Falcon to carry more nose weight than the other models in this series. Try two or more paper clips, to see how they affect its flight. One other built-in oddity of this ship is that it will accept forceful take-offs. Try snapping your wrist when launching it, for an extra-sprightly performance.

Another check on stability and lift can be made by flying the plane through air currents, such as those created by a fan, an air conditioner, or an outdoor breeze. You will begin to appreciate the usefulness of weighty construction in such turbulence. As a matter of fact, the Falcon can be flown like a kite, with a string attached to its nose. With its free-flying capability, this kite-plane can be made to dance on air.

It is interesting to observe how the shapes of the planes influence
their flight characteristics. The Dartmouth Dart follows pretty closely an
arrow's flight, and the wings serve to steer, rather than to support. When
wings are broader and more airfoil-shaped, as in the Flying Tiger and this
Falcon, lift is stronger. Also, there are a flatter glide, greater
stability, and more maneuverability. Reducing the keel and V-shaping also
improves maneuverability, as does increasing the control surfaces.
However, do keep one point in mind. None of this is an exact science.
Fold and fly, but be ready for surprises.

Certain modifications provide new possibilities for maneuverability
of the Falcon:

□ Shorten overall length by starting with an 8½-inch-square sheet
instead of the basic 8½ by 11.

□ Make the keel narrower, or omit it.

□ Feather (bend up) a larger area of the wings—the entire trailing edge
if you don't make a keel.

□ To increase or decrease roll stability, add or eliminate wing V-shapings.

True to its name, the Falcon combines a fast glide with a rock-steady course. An extra
fold along front part of wing provides greater lift and longer flight.

The Pegasus offers wide opportunity for experimentation. By varying wing and tail surfaces, you can make the craft circle or perform intricate stunts.

Paper Folding and Cutting

The Pegasus

The Pegasus is the only two-piece paper airplane in this series, and the most widely variable in its flight characteristics. It can be made to perform a variety of aerobatics. For barrel rolls, launch the plane at high speed, holding it sideways or upside down. For swerves, bend up one wing or a tail trailing edge. Some ships can be made to loop-the-loop by rolling the back edges of the wings upward.

Tail surfaces can be altered in many ways to change performance completely. Make them broader or narrower; crease the rear tabs at different angles. Add elevons by bending up the trailing edges. For greater stability, lengthen the straight section of the tail; for increased maneuverability, shorten it. Add another paper clip to the nose if the plane stalls easily. The original model of this plane, built with a seven-inch tail and with two paper clips on the nose, chalked up a record 50-yard glide.

Folding Instructions

The Pegasus is more complex in design than the other planes described in this article, but is not difficult to make. To build it, follow the directions here, referring to the photographs and figures on these pages.

Following the figures H and F, fold an 8½-by-11-inch sheet of heavy (bond) paper lengthwise along line 1(u). (The letters (u) and (d) indicate whether the fold is up or down.) Open flat; then fold diagonally along line 2(u). Open flat, and fold along line 3(u). Open flat, and fold line 4(d), which passes through the point where lines 1, 2, and 3 intersect. Open paper flat, and refold so that line 4(d) meets the two sides of the paper, as in photograph 12. Press flat.

Fold the top points of this configuration down (photograph 13), so the

F

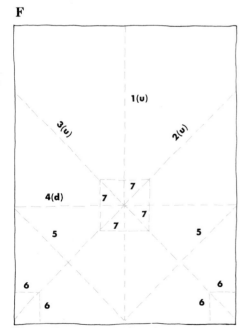

Figure F: Pegasus folding diagram.

G

Figure G: Pattern for Pegasus tail.

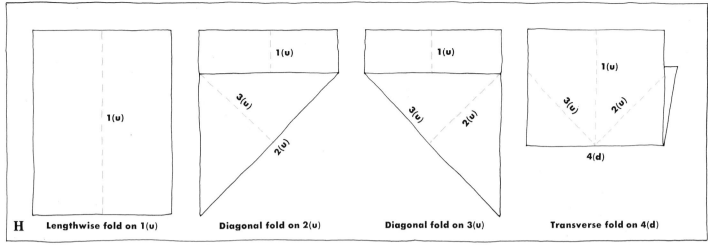

| H | Lengthwise fold on 1(u) | Diagonal fold on 2(u) | Diagonal fold on 3(u) | Transverse fold on 4(d) |

Figure H: Pegasus folding diagram.

creased outer edges rest along the outer edges of the V-shaped paper below. These two folds form the creases marked 5 in figure F, opposite. Cut out the tail piece, figure G, opposite, and insert the point all the way into the nose (photograph 14). Fold back one inch of the nose to hold the tail in place (photograph 15). This last fold forms creases 6 and 7 in figure F. Recrease the keel, and add paper clip at nose.

For related projects and crafts, see "Kite Making," "Origami," and "Oshibana."

12: After making the folds illustrated in figure H, open the paper flat. Gently lift up the sides and press them inward, to form the shape shown here.

13: Fold the upper tips down, as shown, to form two right triangles with the creases lying along the outer edges of the V-shaped paper below them.

14: Insert the cut-out tail piece into the nose, pushing it all the way into the fold. Try making tails of varying lengths, to change flight characteristics.

15: Bend about an inch of the nose back, to hold the tail section in position. Recrease the fold along the centerline of keel, and bend down tail surfaces.

AMERICAN INDIAN CRAFTS
Beadwork and Moccasins

American Indians, regardless of tribe, have a rich art and craft heritage that is second to none in the variety and complexity of its skills. It would take several volumes just to catalog the ancient and modern uses to which these skills have been and are being put.

There are, however, two American Indian handicrafts that are especially popular today: Indian beading and leatherwork. Try to think of a shoe store that doesn't stock moccasin-style footwear. And think of all the beaded headbands, belts, and other Indian-inspired fashion accessories sold all over the world.

To learn to duplicate the authentic Indian-crafted objects of the past would present a unique challenge to ingenuity and intellect. But by following the instructions that begin on the next page, you can make an almost limitless variety of authentic Indian and Indian-inspired beaded accessories—from diamond-shaped rings to daisy-chain necklaces and bracelets—in the designs suggested or in designs you create yourself. You also can make your own moccasins—in both low-top and high-top styles—as the Apache Indians have been making them for hundreds of years.

Alvina Mofsie and her daughter Josephine Tarrant are Indian artisans well-known for their skill in beadwork, which is the craft specialty of their tribe. Born in Nebraska on a Winnebago Reservation, Mrs. Mofsie has lived in New York since 1929. Mrs. Tarrant lives in New Jersey.

Origins of Indian Designs

Designs for authentic Indian motifs for beadwork can be divided into two types, determined by the natural surroundings familiar to the artisans. Woods Indians were the traditional creators of patterns based on flowers, leaves, trees, and animals. When fluid, curved lines appear in Indian work, these also usually can be attributed to tribes from wooded areas. In contrast, the Plains Indians of the American Southwest were inspired by the straight-lined geometric forms of their environment—the flat-topped mesa, for example, and the great desert expanses.

Compared to the leather crafts, beadwork is a relatively new Indian craft, although Indians have been making bead ornaments from shells, bones, seeds, pods, and other natural materials since the earliest times. Beads were also a medium of exchange. Wampum belts, made of beads cut from seashells, had designs that recorded events in the history of the tribe and were used for bartering. But the execution of designs with glass beads began only after the arrival of Europeans, who first brought glass beads to this hemisphere at the time of Columbus. The Europeans traded the beads for the Indians' more valuable furs. In working with glass beads, the Indians translated the traditional designs originally executed by artisans using porcupine quills. This accounts for the straight, geometric lines of much modern beadwork.

Material

Generally, the materials you will need—beads, wire, beeswax, needles, and thread—to make the projects that follow can be purchased at a well-stocked hobby or crafts shop. If there isn't such a shop near you, you should be able to find most, if not all, of the required supplies at the crafts, trimming, notions, stationery counters of any large department store, or even those of five-and-dime stores. Loom beading, of course, requires a simple loom, available at craft shops. Instructions for making one inexpensively yourself are given on page 47.

Beaded medallion, about four inches in diameter, was traditionally worn as an ornament on a headband, a bandolier, or on ceremonial clothes. Project directions are on page 46.

Brilliantly colored geometric motifs of these beaded pieces are typical designs of the American Plains Indians. Work such as this is generally made on a loom and then sewed to fabric or leather.

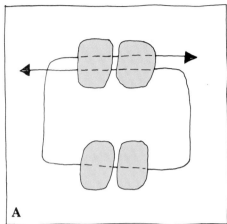

Figure A: First step in making a ring.

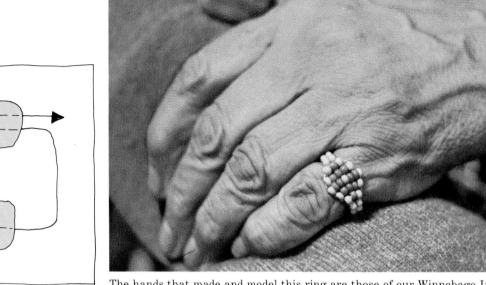

The hands that made and model this ring are those of our Winnebago Indian artisan Alvina Mofsie. The same technique also can be used to make bracelets and necklaces.

1: String a blue bead, an orange bead, and another blue bead on the right-hand wire. Pass the left-hand wire through all three beads; then pull both wires slowly in opposite directions. Take care not to kink wires when pulling.

2: String a blue bead, three orange beads, and another blue bead on the right-hand wire. Pass the left-hand wire through all five beads, and pull both wires until the new row is neatly set against the three-bead row below.

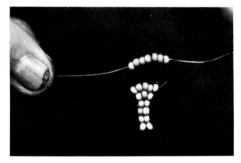

3: String a blue bead, two orange beads, another blue bead, two more orange beads, and a last blue bead on the right-hand wire. Put the left-hand wire through all seven beads, and pull. At this point, the ring is more than half completed.

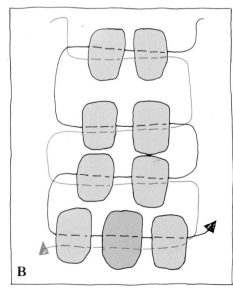

Figure B: Finishing a beaded ring.

Jewelry, Lapidary and Metalwork
Beaded ring

Although Indians generally did not wear beaded rings, the designs used for bracelets, headbands, and bandoliers do make attractive rings.

Making the Ring

□ Cut an 18-inch length of No. 30 stainless-steel wire, and string two blue beads to its center. See figure A.

□ Then string two blue beads on the right-hand wire. Pass the left-hand wire through both beads, and pull wires slowly—wire kinks easily—in opposite directions. See figure A.

□ Continue stringing two blue beads at a time until the chain, placed under your ring finger, reaches the sides of your finger.

□ Follow the instructions given with photographs 1, 2, and 3 above. Then repeat the steps described for photographs 2 and 1, in that order.

□ Now all you have to do is join the ends of the diamond-shape ring by passing the wires through the beads as shown in figure B.

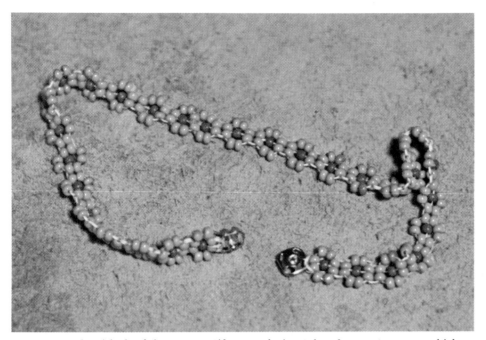

Necklace made with the daisy as a motif uses a design taken from nature, one which often appears in the work of contemporary American Indian artisans.

Mass-produced seed beads are often uneven in size and shape. Mrs. Mofsie takes great care to select only uniform beads for her daisy chain.

Jewelry, Lapidary and Metalwork
Beaded daisy chain

The daisy is a traditional Indian motif which here is incorporated in a chain. Once you have grasped the basic technique you can adapt it to make necklaces, bracelets, and earrings. Daisy ornaments also can be appliqued to fabric or leather.

Instructions for Making Daisy Chain
□ Draw thread hard across block of beeswax, and thread the needle. Double the thread over, and knot the ends together.
□ String eight blue beads, and go back through first bead. See figure C1, which illustrates the process.
□ Add an orange bead, and go through bead A. See figure C2.
□ Add blue beads C, D, and go back through beads B, A, C, D. See figure C3.
□ Add six blue beads, and go through bead C. See figure C4.
□ Repeat steps 3, 4, and 5 until daisy chain is of desired length.
□ Sew ends together, or add snaps or hook and eye.

The orange center bead (see also figure C2 below) matches in size and harmonizes with the surrounding blue beads of the daisy-chain petals.

▼ Figure C: The four steps used in making the daisy chain.

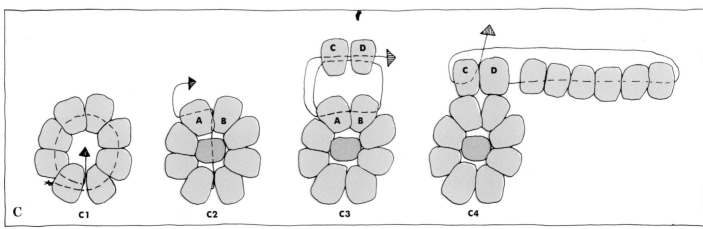

C   C1   C2   C3   C4

Jewelry, Lapidary and Metalwork
Medallion

To make a medallion, you need bead graph paper, two No. 10 needles, No. 50 mercerized-cotton thread, beeswax, a No. 110 needle, thin, stiff cardboard, and two pieces of felt slightly larger than your medallion.

On graph paper, plot your own design or that of the medallion on page 42. Thread the needle; double the thread; knot; beeswax. Follow figure D.

Next, string and lay out the first plotted ring. Then, as shown in figure E, pass the needle back through A, B, and send it down next to B. Bring the needle back up half a bead width from B, ready for stringing the second ring. Thread the second needle; double thread; knot; beeswax. Send it up between center bead and D, E. Then send it down to tack, D, E. Repeat at F, G, so that all beads are tacked in groups of two (A and B are already secured). Tack all succeeding rings the same way.

After following the instructions for photographs 4 through 7, you will have a medallion to hang from, or stitch to, anything you would like to decorate. See "Beadwork" entry for specific instructions on tacking.

▲ Young Kevin Tarrant wears headband and necklace ornamented with medallions.

▼ Medallion incorporating daisy motif is decorated with shells.

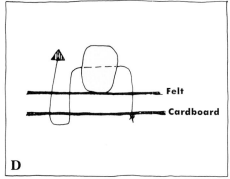

D

Figure D: Glue cardboard to back of square of felt and sew bead through the center.

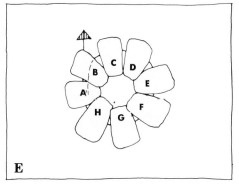

E

Figure E: Use both beading and tacking needles to secure rings, as shown above.

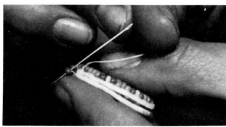

4: Each ring must be closely inspected for design conformity before it is tacked down. Seed beads too large or too small can destroy the symmetry of the design.

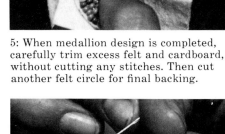

5: When medallion design is completed, carefully trim excess felt and cardboard, without cutting any stitches. Then cut another felt circle for final backing.

6: The second felt backing is sewed on with a finishing stitch that makes a gay border around the medallion. String three beads, and send the needle from rear to front.

7: Catch the front bead (the last bead strung), and pull until the center bead stands straight up. Repeat, using two beads, until border has been completed.

Jewelry, Lapidary and Metalwork
Loom beading

8: Four pieces of scrap wood and eight nails are materials needed to make loom.

9: To string loom, tie No. 8 cotton thread around sidepiece end.

10: After winding as many strings as you will use, tie thread again to sidepiece.

11: With your fingers, gently space warp threads a bead width's distance apart.

12: Thread No. 12 needle with No. 50 cotton thread. Double; tie to outer warp.

13: String beads, and position them underneath and between the warp threads.

14: Gently push beads up above the warp threads, and pass needle through them.

15: Tying ends is easy with an even number of warp threads. Just pair them, and knot.

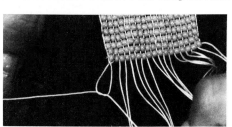

16: To finish the piece, tape ends, and fold them under where they won't be seen.

Many American Indian beadwork pieces are made on a loom, which allows the artisan to work with several strands of beading at once. A beading loom is simply a rectangle consisting of four pieces of wood nailed together.

The loom used to illustrate the looming technique of beading, photograph 8, was made from 18-by-1½-by-½-inch and 6-by-3-by-¾-inch pieces of wood. You can use wood of any length and width as long as the finished loom is sturdy, level, and longer and wider than the beadwork you wish to create. Make sure that the side-pieces are low enough to allow you to reach over them to work under the warp threads strung lengthwise on the loom.

Loom-beaded works can be belts, necklaces, headbands, even cat collars. They can be sewed on shirts, dresses, jeans, and jackets, or they can stand on their own merits without any material backing.

Work with a Graph

For your first loom-beading project, copy any of the American Indian designs shown in this article, or make up one of your own. Once you have decided on a design, the best thing to do is to work it out in color on bead graph paper, or you can use ordinary graph paper, which usually is available where school supplies are sold. After your design has been put on graph paper—one square for each bead—you will have a bead-by-bead color guide for each row to be loomed.

To loom, follow these procedures:

Use beeswax on the weft (crosswise) thread that goes through the needle.

Use an odd number of beads for the rows. This will allow you to use a center bead in your design.

Be sure you have strung one more warp (lengthwise) thread than the number of beads needed in each row.

Knot weft thread to warp thread several inches up on the warp, to keep warp thread ends long enough to be tied off later.

Pull weft thread firmly, but gently. Pulling too tightly would make the edges of your work uneven.

Instructions for loomwork are given with photographs 9 to 16.

47

Leathercraft
Apache moccasins

When man first came to the North American continent, he probably was wearing some sort of leather footwear. In the time between that migration and the advent of white men, the original footwear patterns were adapted to divergent climates and terrains encountered by the Indian nations. Anthropologists believe that the Apache was one of the last Indian tribes to migrate south into what is now the United States, so it is not surprising that some of their high-topped-moccasin patterns resemble Eskimo mukluks—soft boots of sealskin or reindeer skin—and other northern footwear.

I have chosen to describe the making of the low-top, or short-style, Apache moccasin for the following reasons: The soft leather this style requires is easier for the novice to work with than is heavy leather; I have found this moccasin well suited to general wear; and I like its appearance better than that of the high-top variety.

For those who would like a higher moccasin, however, I have described a simple modification of this low style (see page 53).

Some Tips for the Beginner

Three pieces are required for this Apache moccasin: Sole, vamp, and back.

I have found that the most effective way to fit a moccasin perfectly is to make the pieces in that sequence, that is, to make the pattern for a piece only after the preceding piece has been completed. In this way, the pieces are fitted to each other, rather than being cut out all together before being assembled. I measure the vamp piece on my foot without first creating a separate pattern for it. After you have made your first pair, you may develop your own techniques.

When laying out patterns on leather, check both sides of the hide carefully, to be sure you are not including scratches, holes, or thin spots. Try to lay out two corresponding pieces—both soles, for example—side by side in the same direction on the hide. This ensures uniform stretch. Do not cut on the bias (that is, with the pattern laid so that the line from heel and toe runs on the diagonal of the hide—see craftnote).

Most important: Try on the moccasin frequently as you are making it. Fittings help you understand how to proceed.

Tools

Besides the leather (see Craftnotes, page 52), you need only a few tools and supplies to make the moccasins shown here.

Marking implements: Felt-tip and ballpoint pens; pencils.

Needles: Straight, sturdy needles, 2 ½ inches or longer. Sewing centers sell hand-stitching needles.

Hand-stitching thread: Stout nylon or waxed linen. It can be bought at shoe-repair and leather shops or in the leather district of a big city.

Awl or fid: Used to make holes through which needle and thread run. It must be very thin and needle-sharp at the tip. I use a carpenter's awl.

Cutting tools: A matte knife, or a replaceable block knife, and a wooden board to cut on are used by many professional leatherworkers. Good, sharp scissors are needed to cut leather. Don't use cheap scissors.

Measuring tools: A tape measure and a straight-edged ruler.

Brown wrapping paper: For patterns.

Old leather glove: To protect your hand as you tighten stitches.

Pliers: To pull the needle through tight spots. Usually, if you can't pull the needle through by hand, the awl hole isn't large enough.

Stephen LePage, Vietnam veteran and former supervisor for a leathercraft factory, lives in Shoreham, Vt., with his wife, Lassie. The LePages grow organic vegetables, raise organic beef, make their own footwear, and work at living off the land.

17: Tools: Pliers; felt-tip pen; ballpoint pen, and pencils; carpenter's awl or a fid, used to enlarge holes; scissors; knife of replaceable-blade type; tape measure; brown paper; wooden board; needles; nylon thread; waxed linen thread; leather glove to protect hands when you are pulling the thread through the holes made by the awl.

The design of these leather moccasins made in the style of the Apache Indian originated with the Eskimo. Apaches migrated to the Southwest from Canada about 1200 A.D.

18: Add a ¾-inch margin to the original tracing of the outline of your foot, as shown here. Lean your full weight on your foot when you trace its outline.

19: As you cut the pattern for the moccasin sole, work close to the inside edge of the outer tracing line. Make the cut edge of the leather close to vertical.

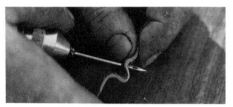

20: With the awl, enlarge each hole for puckering thread. Make holes ⅛ inch apart and ⅛ inch from edge of the sole.

▶ Figure F: The sole. Line A-B is midway.

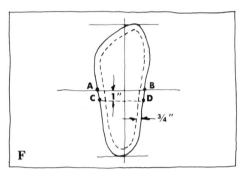

F

Making the Sole

Start by tracing the outline of your foot on a piece of brown wrapping paper. Keep the pen vertical, to get an accurate outline. Add a ¾-inch margin to the foot outline (see figure F), and cut out the pattern. Trace it on the sole leather and then cut the sole out, following this outline.

To shape the leather to your foot, it is necessary to thread a drawstring around the perimeter of the sole piece and draw the edge up about your foot, so that the leather puckers. Holes for the drawstring should be ¼ inch apart and ¼ inch from the edge of the sole. Mark the holes with the point of the awl, then press the awl through the holes. Enlarge each hole with the awl until the needle slides through easily.

Use a four-foot length of thread for the puckering process. Thread the drawstring through the holes, starting at point A and finishing at point A in figure F. To pucker the leather, pull hard on the thread. Wet the leather slightly after it has been threaded, to help mold it to your foot. Use a damp sponge, and do not soak the sole, just moisten it.

Shape the sole around your foot. It should fit your foot without binding your toes. The height of the sides of the sole should be equal all around. Tie threads together on the inside, leaving the ends uncut.

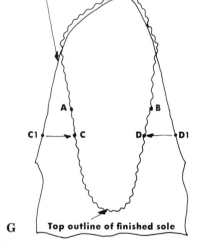

Figure G: Untrimmed vamp laid out flat.

21: As you sew, stop every two inches, and pull hard on the thread, to pucker sole edge. Start stitching at point A in figure F, and finish at point A.

22: Puckered sole is fitted to your foot after thread has been laced completely around edge. Wet the leather with a damp sponge, to help mold it to your foot.

23: Notice here that the thread is tightly drawn at the points of maximum curvature, which shows the most pucker. Thread is only slightly drawn along the sides.

Making the Moccasin Top (Vamp)

On the sole piece, determine points shown as A, B, C, D, in figure **G**. Make a light pen mark at each. Points C, D, are about one inch back from A, B. From your vamp material (see Craftnotes, page 52), cut a piece as long as your foot and twice as wide. Put your foot down on the puckered sole. Lay vamp leather over the foot, and press vamp leather hard against sole edge, to make an impression. Turn the vamp piece over, and trace the sole's impression with your pen. Figure **G** is a sketch of vamp leather with points A, B, C, D, inked in to correspond to sole markings. Draw lines on the vamp piece at right angle to C, D, extending to vamp-piece edges, and draw lines from outer edges of toes to meet these lines at C₁ and D₁. Cut out the vamp.

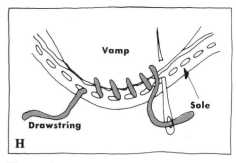

Figure **H**: Whip stitch used to bind sole and vamp pieces. As you work, enlarge every other drawstring hole in the sole, and punch holes in the vamp above sole hole.

24: A piece of vamp material the length of your foot and twice its width is pressed against puckered sole firmly enough to mark the vamp leather.

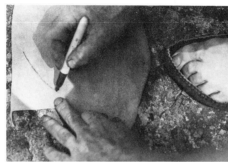

25: Ink the outline made on the vamp underside from tips of toes back to points C, D on figure **G**. It will be clear if you press firmly.

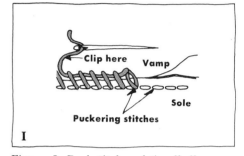

Figure **I**: Backstitch and tie off all threads on the inside of the moccasin: tying off process is essential if the moccasin is to be long-lasting and sturdy.

26: With sole and vamp lined up at A, B, C, D, make reference marks on edge of each. This will help you keep pieces lined up when you sew them together.

27: Photograph shows a row of tight, even stitches, and this is your objective: careful sewing that gives a professional look to the finished moccasins.

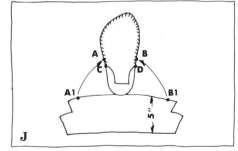

Figure **J**: Back piece of the moccasin. Note that it is slightly curved to fit your heel more closely at the top. Distance A₁, B₁ equals distance AB measured around heel.

Attaching and Trimming the Vamp

When you have cut out the vamp, it should resemble figure **G**. Check for fit by laying it on your foot. When you pull up the sole edges to meet the vamp, you should have a tight fit across the ball of your foot and a bit of slack around arch and instep, at C, D. Trim vamp if it is too large.

With sole and vamp on your foot, make ink marks along the cut edges of both at several points, so you can keep pieces lined up as you sew. Thread a four-foot length, and use the whipstitch, figure **H**. Begin at toe. At the first stitch, pull through half the thread; the rest is reserved for the other half of the seam. Pull stitches tight; wear glove, to protect your hand. When you get to point C, or D, tie off the thread, as shown in figure **I**. Thread needle with reserved thread, and sew other side. Tie off.

Put on the moccasin, smooth the vamp, and mark and trim it, as in figure **J**. When fitting the vamp, let it lie smoothly against your instep; don't pull it to either side. When finished, vamp should taper smoothly from C to a width of about three inches at the top. Mistakes in trimming aren't crucial, since the cuts will be covered by the flaps of the back piece.

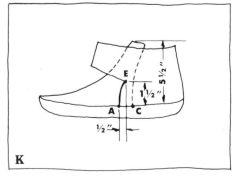

Figure **K**: Sidecuts A. E, (and B, F on the other side of the moccasin) are made after the back piece has been attached to the moccasin.

LEATHER CRAFTNOTES

The following leathers are listed in the order of their availability and are recommended for making moccasins:
Cowhide: After initial tanning, cowhide is ¼-inch thick and fairly stiff. The tanneries then split it into the desired weights of top grain and suede splits (suede on both sides). The standard unit of leather thickness is the ounce. One ounce equals 1/64 inch. After being split, leather is processed for color, flexibility and surface texture.
Vesting Leather: These moccasin tops are made of vesting leather.
Soft Bag Leather: Similar to vesting leather, but twice as heavy.
Latigo and Other Oil-tanned Leathers: I use it for all my moccasin soles. Light, strong, and moisture-resistant.
Horsehide: Excellent texture and strength, but can be hard to find.
Elk and Moose Hide: Indian materials. If available in correct weight, use it.

Leather Suppliers

Good leather is expensive, but no more so than good fabric. Cowhide costs between fifty cents and one dollar a square foot at this writing—15 to 30 square feet per half hide. Few suppliers will cut up a half hide.

The best and most economical suppliers of high quality leather in small quantities are the jobbers of garment,

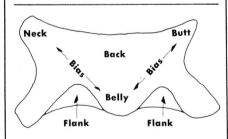

bag, and belt leathers located in the leather districts of large cities. Craftpeople and leather shops usually deal with the leather-district tradesmen. Look in the classified directory of the largest city near you, under the listing "Leather."

Individual leather shops are geared to marketing their own products and are not always willing to sell skins. Most often they sell their scraps already packaged. These packages are something of a gamble, and often the contents are pieces too small to finish a project, or scraps of poor quality are included.

28: The top of the vamp piece should be about three inches wide. It should taper smoothly from points shown as C and D in figure **J**.

29: Marking side edges of the vamp prior to trimming. Note the awl-pierced front edge of the vamp piece. Line shows vamp tapering to a three-inch-wide top.

30: The back piece is now attached to the sole, slightly overlapping the edge of the vamp. Fold outer back-piece flap over vamp first, then inner flap.

31: If the outside flap of the back piece is too long, cut it down to a reasonable, or comfortable, length. The photograph illustrates this process.

Working the Back Piece

The back piece is simple to make and to attach. With a tape, measure from A to B (figure **J**) around the heel. Using this measurement, make a brown-paper pattern as sketched in figure **J**. Notice that the back piece is slightly curved at the heel. After tracing the pattern on leather for the back piece, cut it out and measure a 4-to-5-foot length of thread.

Center the back piece at the rear of the sole, figure **J**. Begin at center, reserving half the thread for the other side of the seam. Stitch A₁, B₁ to points A and B, and then tie off (figure **I**). Parts of the seam, where the back piece overlaps the vamp, will require a little more force to pull thread through. Use pliers if necessary. When the seam is completed, backstitch the drawstring ends, left over from the puckering process, inside the moccasin, and clip off.

Trimming and Finishing the Back

The back-piece flaps affect the fit of the moccasin, so trim them carefully. Figure **K** shows where to trim the back piece to join the vamp; trim from points A to E, and the matching points on other side. Put on the moccasin and fold the outside flap of the back piece over the vamp, as in photograph 30. If this flap is too long (it tucks down into the sole), cut off the end, as shown in photograph 31. Now fold the other flap over it.

Stretch a string tightly across the instep from point E, in figure **K** to the matching point on the opposite side of the moccasin, corresponding to point E. Both flaps should be trimmed so that their lower edges fall along the line delineated by the string. Next, from scrap leather cut a lace ⅛ inch wide and about 18 inches long. With your matte knife, make lacing holes an inch above the sole seam. Each pair of lacing holes should be far enough back so the lace will cross the flaps. See photographs 32 and 33. Notch the upper flap as shown in photograph 34.

High-Top Version of the Apache Moccasin

Here is a variation on this basic design actually used by the Apache. The following instructions refer to figure L.

Sole Piece: Identical to that for the low-cut moccasin.

Vamp Piece: Same as short version, but when you have traced the pattern as far as C_1 and D_1 —figure G, page 50 (marked as X and Y on figure L here)— the side edges are parallel.

Back Piece: Rectangular. The width is equal to distance C_1 and D_1, figure L, measured around the heel, with an extra inch or so added for a margin of error, to give leeway when you are attaching back to sole. Unneeded material will be trimmed off.

The following sequence is suggested for making the high-top version:

Make sole, as before.

Attach vamp, as before, to C_1 and D_1, figure L, around toe.

Using the glover's stitch, figure M, attach the vamp at Y, figure L, to the back piece at C_2, and sew up the side to T and U.

Starting at C_2, sew bottom of the back piece to the sole.

When this seam meets the other side of the vamp, at X, trim off the unused portion of the margin-of-error material.

Turn the moccasin inside out, and sew the remaining side seam, from X and D_2 to S and V.

Cut off the top edge so that it is even, and fold down inside to make a hem, if desired.

Traditional Indian ceremonial moccasins were decorated with quillwork or beading. You may wish to imitate these intricate techniques by adapting information and designs in the beadwork section of this article.

Lassie putting the last stitches on a pair of high-top moccasins. Frequent fittings while the moccasins are being made guarantee a comfortable fit.

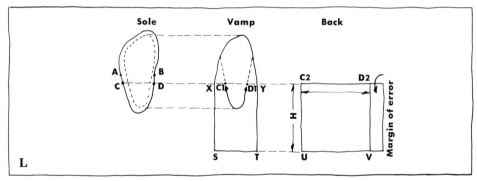

Figure L: Steps in making the high-top moccasin parallel steps for low-top version. Distance between C_1, D_1, measured around the heel, equals distance C_2, D_2.

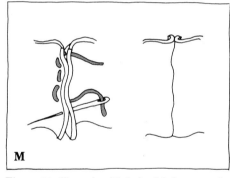

Figure M: Glover's stitch for high-top style.

For additional crafts and projects, see "Basketry," "Beadwork," "Belts and Buckles," "Canoeing," "Carryalls," "Flowers, Artificial," "Jewelry," "Leather Braiding," "Mineralogy," "Pottery," "Sandalmaking," "Shelters," "Silvercraft," "Survival Techniques," "Tooling," "Totem Poles," "Vegetable Dyes," "Weaving."

32: Laces for your moccasins are cut ⅛-inch wide from scrap leather. They should be about 18 inches long. Lacing holes are made in pairs and lie an inch above sole seam.

33: The lace must pass over both back-piece flaps, holding them securely in place. Here, the upper flap is marked for notching, which will keep flaps from shifting.

34: View of the notch being cut to keep moccasin flaps in place. Notch is cut into the upper flap beneath the area where the lace will pass.

ANIMAL DOLLS
Fantasy in Toys

Stanley Dunaj, Art Director of the Promotion Department of Popular Mechanics *magazine, has designed covers for* Young Readers Press *and* Family Weekly *and has illustrated children's books. He is a graduate of Cooper Union in New York City.*

Stuffed animals and dolls, in their own comfortable, cuddly, and often clumsy way, have a special appeal for children. In fact, they have an elusive quality, derived from their creation by loving hands, that is seldom achieved in manufactured toys. Since ancient times, children have treasured the unique personalities of their homemade dolls and animals. Throughout the historic turmoils of Europe and, subsequently, of pioneer America, Raggedy Anns and simply crafted stuffed animals have been cherished members of every growing household.

Stuffed animals, like stuffed or cloth dolls, can be made from bits and pieces of material at hand and constructed to resemble their real counterparts or such fantasy animals as Piglet, Heffalump, and Kanga and Roo, of Winnie-the-Pooh fame.

The teddy bear, a staple in every child's cache of toys, was suggested by a 1903 Washington-newspaper cartoon depicting Theodore Roosevelt's refusal, while on a bear hunt, to shoot a cub. Inspired by this cartoon, Morris Michtom, a Brooklyn toy-store owner, made a small brown bear of plush, with shoe-button eyes. The cub was named Teddy in honor of Roosevelt, and millions of teddy bears have been manufactured since.

Animals' appeal to children is irresistible and universal. What child could resist a tawny lion with a full, dark mane framing his catlike face? Or a big gray elephant with huge, flopping ears and swaying, sinuous trunk? Or how about an alligator with a triangular snout, long

scaly body, and short sturdy feet? I have created stuffed versions of these curious creatures. These pages show how easily they can be made.

When you present a child with one of these lovable animals, tell or write him a story with your own embellishments and variations on basic plots. For instance, there are countless stories about the elephant's memory, but the one about the elephant who went mad is my favorite. It seems that an elephant suddenly lost control and went racing about trampling people. But when he saw a lady and her child, who had been in the habit of feeding him every day, he stopped instantly and gently lifted both lady and child to safety before continuing his wild stampede. Or how about this story? An elephant asserted that he was the strongest animal on earth, and an alligator answered that he was the strongest animal in the swamp. They fought for days, but neither would give in, so the battle was declared a draw. Both alligator and elephant claimed victory—the elephant on land, the alligator in the swamp. Ah Lee, my little stuffed alligator, is not an elephant fighter, but he's fun to have around.

Materials Needed for Stitching Animals

For all the animals, use any scraps of fabric available. They will look as well dressed in the thin cotton of an old apron as they will in leftover scraps of drapery material. Felt can be purchased in 12-by-9-inch pieces. The yarn can be new or used, but for the mane of the lion, I prefer used wool, which is curly and makes a cuddlier animal. Novelty buttons can be purchased in a local notions shop or rescued from old clothing. For fill, you can use a polyester stuffing. On all pattern diagrams, the symbols have the same meaning: A solid line indicates the cutting line; a broken line indicates the sewing line; a row of Xs indicates the position of additional pieces; also, X marks button placement.

Children of all ages love stuffed animals, and seven-year-olds like Holly Hunter can help make them. Here, Holly is engrossed in stuffing—the final step that will turn stitched pieces of fabric into Ah Lee, an alligator with a personality. (See page 62.)

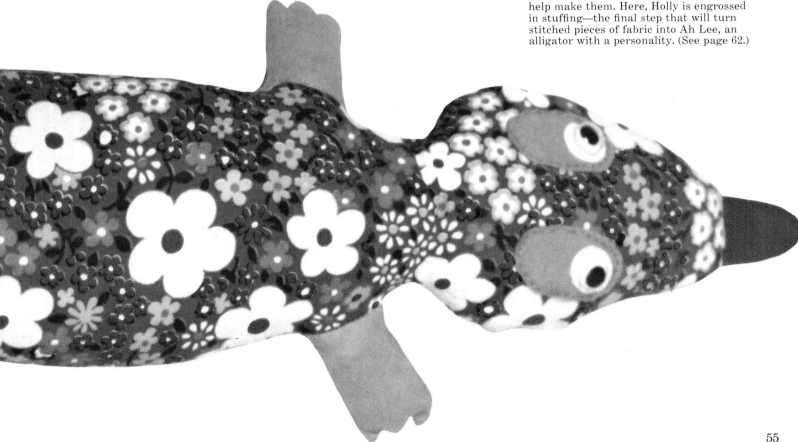

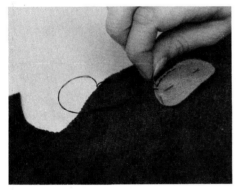

1: Place the two pieces of fabric with right sides together. Pin the pattern to the fabric along the sewing line (the broken line) at intervals of about five inches. Cut out around pattern along the cutting line (the solid line).

2: Backstitching is easy as an attractive and sturdy finish for felt pieces. Draw needle up from bottom. Insert it ¼ inch behind thread, and come out ¼ inch ahead.

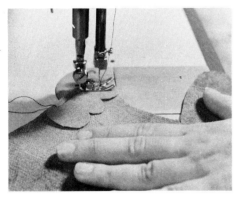

3: You can use machine top stitching as an alternative to hand stitching. On Heffa, the elephant, regular-size (12) machine stitches were used to outline the toes and show the separations between them.

Heffa, the lumpy elephant

Elephants are truly enormous beasts. African elephants, with their very large ears and heavy ivory tusks, can weigh over seven tons. Indian elephants, the kind we see most often in zoos, are smaller. Both kinds are extremely strong and in some countries have been trained to be beasts of burden. They can easily travel 50 to 60 miles a day and, when urged, 100 miles. Elephants live 100 to 200 years, and their memories are said to be just as long-lived. I named my stuffed elephant Heffa.

To make Heffa, you will need two pieces of identical fabric, each measuring at least 20 by 14 inches. Any weight will be fine. Six pieces of felt are needed—four matching the color of the body fabric, one red for the mouth, one blue for centers of the eyes. The tail is made from 12 strands of yarn (any weight) at least 12 inches long. And you'll need material for stuffing—cotton, filament filling, or shredded foam.

On paper divided into ½-inch squares, enlarge (see page 57) all elements shown in figure A. Include all lines and other marks. Cut pattern.

Place the two pieces of fabric with right sides together. Pin on pattern (see photograph 1), and cut out two body sections. Use felt matching the body for the ears. Cut out four. Use the same color felt for eyes (cut out two) and toes (cut out four). Cut out two small eye sections in blue felt and two mouth sections in red felt. After all pieces are cut out, transfer markings from pattern pieces onto the cloth and felt.

Now you are ready to begin construction. With a double strand of matching thread, sew large sections of eyes onto head sections. Backstitching is excellent if you are handsewing—it will give a sturdy, neat finish. (Felt pieces can be sewed on by machine unless otherwise stated.) Sew small eye pieces onto large ones. By hand or machine, sew a mouth half to each body half. Sew on toes, top stitching the *(continued)*

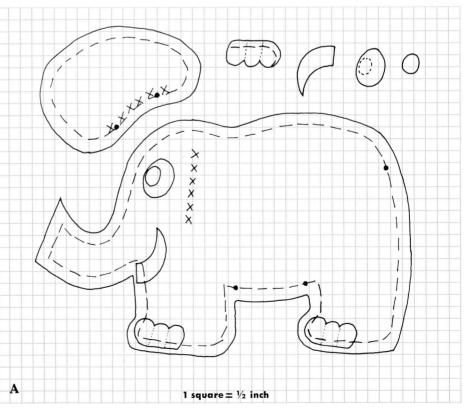

A

1 square = ½ inch

Figure A: Pattern for Heffa, the lumpy elephant.

CRAFTNOTES ON ENLARGING PATTERNS

Throughout the volumes of The Family Creative Workshop, patterns are reproduced for you to copy. To make a pattern full size, follow the system described here for enlarging the grid imposed on the heart pattern.

The system is really very simple. The small grid in the book must be translated onto a grid with larger squares that you will make; the design (in this case, the heart) will be copied onto this larger grid. The size of the enlarged grid you make will depend on what the pattern is for. For example, for a pillow pattern the grid will have much smaller squares than will a grid for a tablecloth or a bedspread. A gauge is given with each pattern printed. Draw the squares of the large grid you prepare to the size given by this gauge.

Before you cut your pattern, be sure an allowance has been made for seams.

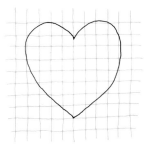

Above is the pattern of a heart as it might appear in these volumes. The grid placed over it is divided into small squares that actually measure ⅛ inch. All the patterns in the Creative Workshop use grids of this size. On the opposite page, the pattern for Heffa, the elephant, is reproduced on such a ⅛-inch grid. To make a pattern that will produce Heffa in the size pictured, you must transfer the pattern for Heffa onto a grid whose squares are ½ inch in size, as noted with the pattern.

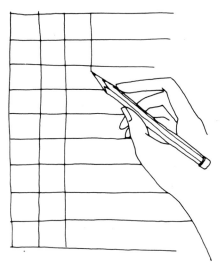

To enlarge the Heffa pattern, prepare a grid that has the same number of squares as our illustrated grid for the elephant, but one in which each square measures ½ inch on each side.

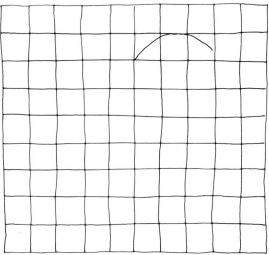

Draw pattern onto your ½-inch grid a square at a time.

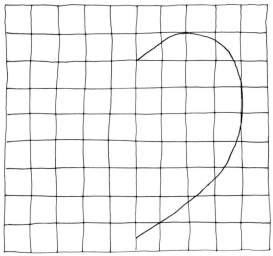

Follow the lines around, checking the book as you go.

You will find it easy to transfer the whole pattern.

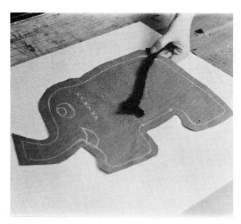

4: Position knotted end of braided tail on Heffa's body at dot on rear on right side of fabric. Be sure knot is between the stitching line and the cut edge. Have the rest of the tail extended across the elephant's body.

5: Once tail is positioned, use a basting stitch, at the knot, to secure it to Heffa's body temporarily. When the body sections are sewed together, the tail will be anchored by the seam. Double stitch the seam here, for extra strength.

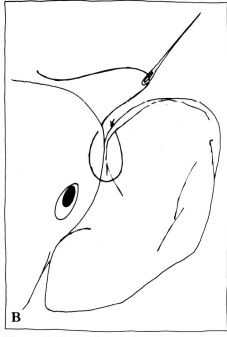

Figure B: Use whip stitch to sew on ears after Heffa is stuffed. Inner curve of ear will match the curve on the stuffed body.

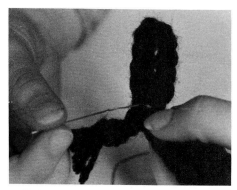

6: Heffa is an elephant with a curly tail, and here is how the curl is put in. First, make a loop in the tail. With a double strand of thread, matching the tail's color, sew the tail at the point where the braid crosses itself. Conceal the thread stitches in the yarn.

7: After the eyes, mouth, toes, and tail have been sewed to the right side of Heffa, place body pieces together, right sides facing, and sew the seam all around, leaving the space between the dots (on the belly) open. Turned right side out, this is where he is stuffed.

markings for each toe. Now construct the tail. Divide 12 strands of yarn into groups of four, and braid as you would hair (see figure C), only begin by tying a knot at one end. Hand stitch loose ends to keep braid from unraveling. Baste knotted end of the tail to the right side of either half of Heffa's body. Do this at the dot on the rear. The major part of the tail should be lying across the body (see photograph 4). The tail will be sewed permanently in place with the seam.

With the right sides of the body together and the tail between them, sew along stitching line, leaving an opening between dots at the belly. Trim seam allowances to ¼ inch around elephant, except where the opening is. Clip all curved seam edges (see figures G and H, page 62). Turn elephant right side out, and stuff. Close opening with hand stitches. Now put the curl in the tail. Make a loop, and stitch it together where the tail overlaps. Next, construct the ears. Sew two pieces of felt together for each ear. Do this along the stitching line, leaving an opening between the dots. Trim seam to ¼ inch, and clip curved edges. Turn ear right side out, and stuff. Hand stitch the opening closed. Sew the ears onto the body by hand also, as it would be impossible to do this by machine. Match the Xs on the ear to the Xs on the body. Use a double strand of thread for strength. Now Heffa, the elephant, is complete. Bring on the peanuts!

◄ Security at bedtime is Heffa, the lumpy elephant, a cuddly beast who whispers funny stories in the dark, but has the deplorable habit of discarding peanut hulls between the sheets.

▼ Figure C: Making an elephant's tail is as easy as braiding hair. Take 12 strands of yarn at least 12 inches long. Tie a knot at one end; then braid for five inches.

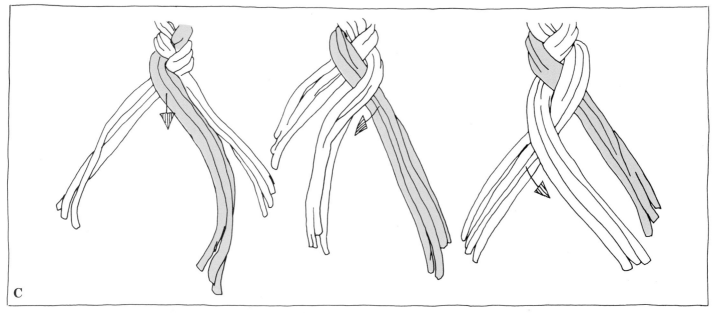

C

Needlecrafts
Lou, the blue-maned lion

Children (and adults) have always been in awe of the strength, majesty, and undaunted courage of the lion, King of the Jungle. A full-grown lion may measure ten feet from nose to tail tip and a lioness a foot less. Lions fiercely stalk their prey at night, but both male and female are very solicitous of their young. The lioness ordinarily bears a litter of two or, at most, three cubs and nurses them for perhaps a year. The young lions mature in about five years, and they live about 70 years.

Medieval knights respected the lion's valor and chose his image for their shields and arms. Remember the bravery of England's Richard I (1157-1199) and his nickname, Richard the Lion-Hearted? I call my stuffed lion Lou. Here is all the information you need to bring him into being.

How To Put Your Lion Together
You will need two pieces of identical fabric (any weight) measuring 20 by 20 inches each; two pieces of felt, a blue for eyes, nose, and mouth, and a green for ears; two novelty buttons (hearts) for the eyes; for the tail end, two ounces of wool (any weight); for the mane, unraveled blue yarn; for whiskers, four pipe cleaners. You also need stuffing material.

After making patterns (figure E), cut out pieces. Cut out two each of body and leg sections, from same fabric. Cut out two eyes, a nose, and a mouth from blue felt, and four ears from green felt.

8: Narrowness of the tail may make it difficult to stuff. Stuff as much from inside the body as possible. Then, using a blunt object, such as the end of a pen or the eraser end of a pencil, stuff from the opening at the end of the tail.

9: Woolly tail end is easy to make from either new (straight) or curly (unraveled) yarn. Make 30 six-inch pieces. Use one strand to tie the rest at the center.

10: After the center is tied securely, fold the tail in half at that point. The tail end is now three inches long and is ready to be attached to the main tail.

11: Turn in the edge of the main tail ¼ inch. Make sure the stuffing reaches this point. Poke the center of the yarn tail into the main tail as far as possible.

12: To keep it in place, stitch the yarn tail to the main tail. Use a double thread of a matching color. You will have to use hand stitches, since this is an awkward job. It will take several firm stitches to keep Lou's tail in place.

Begin construction by sewing the leg sections to the body, placing the right side of the legs facing the right side of the body. Stitch along the curved sides only—that is, around the legs themselves. Do not stitch the straight edge. Do this for both halves of the body. Place the right sides of the two halves together, and sew these sections together. Begin at the front dot on the straight edge of the leg section; continue across and up the head, along the back, and stop at the dot on the upper part of the tail. Now start at the dot at the back of the straight edge of the leg section, and sew the rear, stopping at the dot on the bottom part of the tail. This leaves two openings—one between the front and rear legs and one at the end of the tail. Trim the seam allowances to ¼ inch. Clip all curved seam edges (page 62). Turn Lou right side out.

Now sew on the features. Sew on the eyes, nose, and mouth by hand; it would be impossible to sew them by machine. Sew the buttons onto the felt eyes. Construct the ears. For each ear, use two pieces of felt. Sew ears along the stitching line, leaving the straight edge open. Use

Lou, the blue-maned lion, pretends he is King of the Beasts. Actually, he's gentle as a lap dog. The curly mane comes not from a bad temper, but from unraveled yarn ends.

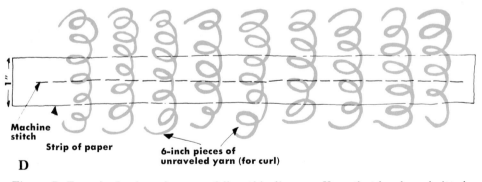

D

1"

Machine stitch

Strip of paper

6-inch pieces of unraveled yarn (for curl)

Figure D: To make Lou's curly mane, follow this diagram. Yarn that has been knitted, steamed with an iron, and allowed to dry thoroughly, will be permanently curled.

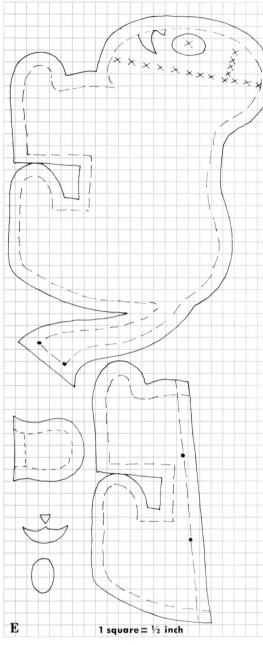

E   1 square = ½ inch

Figure E: Pattern for Lou, the lion.

machine stitches for this. Trim the seams to ¼ inch, and clip the curved edges. Turn right side out, and stuff. Do not close the openings now. Combine two steps: Close ear openings while sewing the ears to the head, along the row of Xs over the eye (see Figure E). Use a backstitch (see photograph 2, page 56). Now stuff Lou, and close opening on belly. Use a pin or any narrow object to stuff the tail (see photograph 8). Be sure the first batch of stuffing is poked firmly all the way into the tail end.

Next, make the mane. Cut new (straight) or used (curly and unraveled) yarn into six-inch lengths. Cut a strip of paper an inch wide and long enough to fit around Lou's head along the row of Xs. Sew one end of yarn

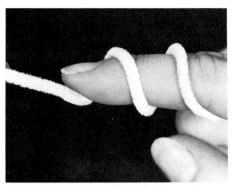

13: Lou's whiskers are made from pipe cleaners. To make them, twist ⅝ of each pipe cleaner around your index finger, leaving ⅜ straight for attaching.

14: Place two whiskers on each side of Lou's nose. Sew them to the face one at a time, using a double thread. Match the thread to the color of the pipe cleaners.

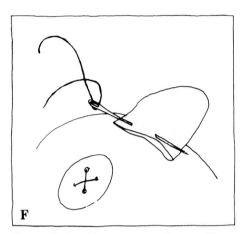

Figure F: Combine two steps in one: Close Lou's ear and sew into the body at the same time. Use thread matching the ear color. Backstitching will give a sturdy finish.

lengths to paper (figure D, page 61). Use a machine stitch and plenty of yarn, for fullness. You may have to make two strips like this. Trim paper close to stitching. Sew the mane by hand onto the head along the row of Xs.

For the tail end, take about 30 strands of six-inch-long yarn, and follow instructions for photographs 9 through 12, page 60.

For the whiskers, wrap ⅝ of a pipe cleaner around your finger, leaving ⅜ free (photograph 13) for attaching to face. Make four, and hand stitch them to the face, two on each side (photograph 14).

Needlecrafts
Ah Lee, the alligator

In the swamps of Florida and Georgia, alligators grow to be as long as ten feet. Keep that in mind the next time you are tempted to buy one of the tiny ones sold in some pet shops. My little stuffed alligator, Ah Lee, promises not to grow. (See photograph, page 54.) Here is how to make him.

You will need two pieces of identical fabric (any weight) measuring 28 by 11 inches each; three pieces of felt, one to match the fabric of the body, one red for the tongue, one white for the eyes; two novelty

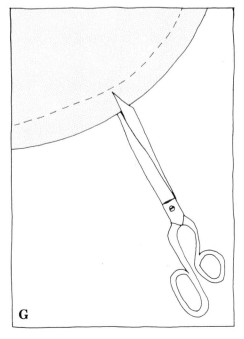

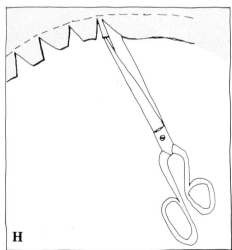

Figure G: For a smooth finish when animals are right side out, clip curved seam edges. On outward curves, make straight slits. Do not cut through the stitching.

Figure H: On inward curves, clip small Vs.

buttons for the eyes; and you need stuffing material. If you wish the tongue to curl, you will need a pipe cleaner.

First, make patterns from grid at right. Then cut top and bottom of Ah Lee's body separately, but use same pattern piece. For bottom, cut along cutting line that includes the feet (do not cut off the feet). But for top, cut along inner cutting line. Cut out two each of the feet and of

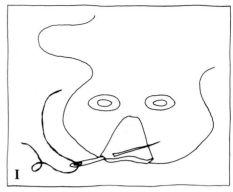

Figure I: Baste tongue to top body piece as shown. It will be sewed in with seam.

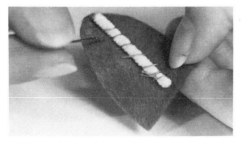

15: To make a tongue with a curl, use a pipe cleaner the length of the tongue. Hand stitch it to one of tongue pieces. Use thread to match the tongue color.

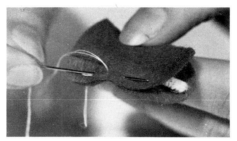

16: Sandwich the pipe cleaner between two pieces of the tongue. With a double strand of matching thread, back stitch the pieces of tongue together.

Holly Hunter, our young animal builder, stuffs the body of an alligator who will soon become Ah Lee, two-foot-long mayor of the friendliest swamp in all Florida.

the large section of the eyes in felt matching the body color. Cut out two small sections of the eyes, in white felt, and two of the tongue, in red felt. Transfer all markings from the patterns to the fabric.

Begin by sewing the large eye sections to the top half of the body, with hand or machine stitches. Then sew small eye sections to large ones where indicated. Sew a button onto each small section. Next, attach the felt feet to the top half of the body. To do this, place the right side of a foot on the right side of the body, matching the notches. Sew along the stitching line; then iron the seam open flat. Do this for each foot.

Next, construct the tongue. Cut a piece of pipe cleaner the length of the tongue. Handsew it to one section of the tongue (see photograph 15). Sew the second piece of tongue to the first, fitting the pipe cleaner between (see photograph 16). Match the dot on the tongue to the one on the top half of the head. Be sure to have the right sides together. Baste the tongue on. At this point, the tip of the tongue should be facing the eyes (see figure I). Place the top body section on the bottom, with the right sides together. Stitch along the stitching line, leaving an opening at the dots between the two left feet. Trim the seam allowance to ¼ inch, and clip all curved seam edges. Turn Ah Lee right side out. Stuff him, and close the opening with invisible hand stitches.

For related projects and crafts, see "Doll Houses and Furniture," "Dolls and Doll Clothes," "Marionettes," "Puppets," "Rag Dolls," "Sewing," "Toys."

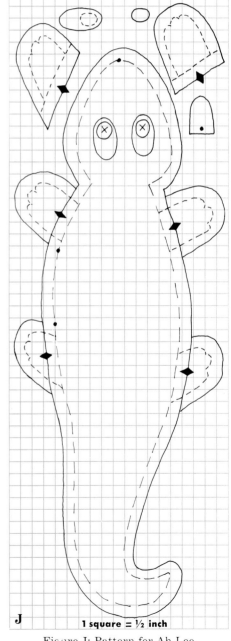

1 square = ½ inch

Figure J: Pattern for Ah Lee.

ANT FARMS
Explore a New World

John C. Pallister, Research Associate of the Department of Entomology of the American Museum of Natural History, in New York, has been on many expeditions to the Amazon Valley and Central America, collecting and identifying insects and studying their ways for the museum. He has coauthored a number of classic works in his field and has also written a book for young people, Following in the Footsteps of the Famous Naturalist, Frank Eugene Lutz.

There are more than 6,500 species of ant, which means that this tiny insect has many thousands of distinct variations. People who study insects are entomologists; those entomologists whose specialty is ants are called myrmecologists. Ants vary in length from an inch to a scant 1/25 inch. They are called social insects because they live in colonies whose members have different jobs to do—foraging for food, caring for the young, breeding, and nest building.

The most important individual in an ant colony is the queen. Her job is to lay eggs, and that she does, hundreds of them, sometimes for as long as 15 years. She can easily be identified by her size, as she is considerably larger than the other ants in her colony. When you dig up an ant nest, you will generally find the queen near the deepest—and most secure—part of it. However, you don't need a queen to start your own ant colony—just a small trowel for digging and one of the two ant houses constructed as described below.

Environmental Projects
Mason-jar ant house

This project, one that a child can manage on his own in an afternoon, provides good training in observation and hours of entertainment. You need only the materials listed under photograph 1. An ant hill will supply the ants—about 100 are needed. Fill both the jar and the bowl about two-thirds full of soil. Set the jar in the bowl, and then set the bowl in the pie plate (figure A on next page). Pour at least an inch of water into the pie plate. The water will serve as a moat to keep the ants from escaping. Don't cover the top of the jar with the metal screw-on cap. You could tie on a piece of cheesecloth, but ants are curious, so let them wander around to see the rest of the world. They will crawl up the inside of the jar, down the outside, and into the bowl for a look-see. They may crawl over the edge of the bowl, but as soon as they reach the water, they will crawl right back. Watch them explore the water with their antennae, just as you might dip your toes into a pool and decide it's too cold to go in.

Ants like variety in their diet and are partial to slices of soft fruit, such as apple or pear, dipped in some sugar water or honey. They also relish bits of meat, cheese, bread, and candy.

Suspend a bit of food, perhaps a sliver of carrot, on a string tied to a pencil. Rest it across the mouth of the jar. If the carrot gets moldy, you can lift it out without disturbing the ants and replace it with other food.

Ants in a Mason-jar farm will climb out to investigate. A bowl of water acts as a moat to prevent their escape. This child's project is made of found materials.

1: Materials for Mason-jar ant house:
Quart-size Mason jar
8-inch soup bowl
10-inch pie plate, 2 inches deep
Short length of string
Pencil or small stick
Soil, water, food, and ants

Fill a Mason jar ⅝ full with soil

Fill a bowl with soil, set jar in bowl

Put an inch of water into pan for a moat

Set jar and bowl in pan

A

2: Collect ants at the ant hill by letting them climb on a pencil. Tap the pencil against the jar rim to dislodge them.

◀ Figure A: Mason-jar ant house.

Add a teaspoonful of water to the soil in the jar every third day; ants need water, but do not give them too much. After a day or so, you will see the first tunnels, probably at the bottom because the soil is moist there.

But what about ants? Where do you find them? Try your own back yard. Collect them as shown in photograph 2, or look for a little mound of sand or dry earth with a small hole in the center and a few ants scurrying about. With a small trowel, cut a circle around the mound about the diameter of your jar. Dig out a cylinder of earth, and place it in a newspaper rolled into the shape of a cone, with the bottom folded up to close it. Transfer ants and soil to your ant house. If you can get a queen, so much the better. Without a queen, your ant farm will last four to six weeks, the life span of worker ants.

Environmental Projects
The ant farm

An ant farm will let you study more closely the structure and patterns of activity in a community of ants. All materials needed are listed under photograph 3. Chances are you have everything except ants and the glass: the latter you can buy from a glass dealer for about the price of a pound of butter. Here is how to build the ant farm:

□ Get two rectangular pieces of glass, each about 8 by 12 inches. The exact size is not too important, but the pieces should be identical.
□ Cut a strip of wood to the longer dimension of the glass, for the frame bottom. Cut two wood strips to the shorter dimension of the glass, for the frame sides. The strips should be ⅜ inch thick, so that only a very thin layer of soil will be sandwiched between the glass panes; this allows you to see the ants and their activities clearly.
□ Fasten the side strips to the bottom strip with small nails, to form a three-sided, or U-shaped, frame.
□ Spread glue around the three edges on one side of a glass pane. Place the wooden frame on it, and press gently. See photograph 4.
□ Spread glue on the upper side of the frame. Place the second pane of glass on it, and press gently. Don't overdo the glue, as too much might crack the glass if dampness in the soil expands the wood.
□ Wait until the glue has set—at least an hour—before applying cloth tape around the edges (photograph 5). The tape acts as a shield,

3: Materials for the ant farm:
Two sheets of glass, about 8 by 12 inches
Strips of 38-inch wood cut ¾ inch wide
Strips of 34-inch wood cut ¾ inch wide
Small nails; waterproof glue
Self-adhesive cloth tape, 1 ½ inches wide
One or two roundhead screws
Soil, water, food, ants

keeping soil particles from escaping. It also covers the raw edges of the glass, preventing finger cuts, and gives the farm a finished look.

☐Cut two ¾-inch-thick wood strips for stand. Cut each one about five inches long, and make a notch in the center (photograph 6). Cut each notch as wide as the farm is thick and about ½ inch deep.

☐The farm also needs a cover. The wooden one shown is for nighttime use. Ants do not need much air, but they do require some. To give them a little more in the daytime, you might make a boxlike cardboard cover slightly larger than the open end. Or you can wad absorbent cotton into the opening loosely enough to allow some air. A piece of cheesecloth tied around the top is another solution.

The best time to collect ants is when a colony is swarming. No one knows what causes ants to swarm. It could be that the original colony becomes too big. At any rate, a swarming signal is given and the workers (who are neuters) push males and females out for the mating flight. (Their wings develop solely for this flight. The males usually die after mating.) Watch for the queen, who is the largest: after the flight, she will pull off her wings and begin to nest. She will lay a few eggs and care for the young until they become workers. After that, she simply lays eggs.

It is easiest to dig up a nest after a rain. The wet soil will hold together and will help keep the ants in the nest. Try to collect about 100 ants, but only from one colony. If you mix ants from two nests, they will fight and eventually will kill each other.

Fill the ant farm about two-thirds full of soil, and add two teaspoonfuls of water. In addition to the food mentioned before, you can sprinkle sugar, birdseed, corn kernels, or bits of cucumber on the soil. Cover, and place the farm in a dark spot in your home or in a cardboard box.

The daily life of the ant becomes more visible because of the narrow structure of this sophisticated ant farm. The colony will last longer if it includes a queen.

4: Use glue sparingly on front and back of a wood frame, to sandwich it between glass.

5: Wide cloth tape covers the edges of glass and frame. Trim corners neatly.

6: Rectangular notches are cut into two small wood strips to make a stand.

7: Spoon ant-soil mixture into the farm. Add a little water only if soil is very dry.

8: A screw makes a good handle for a loose lid that keeps the ants from wandering.

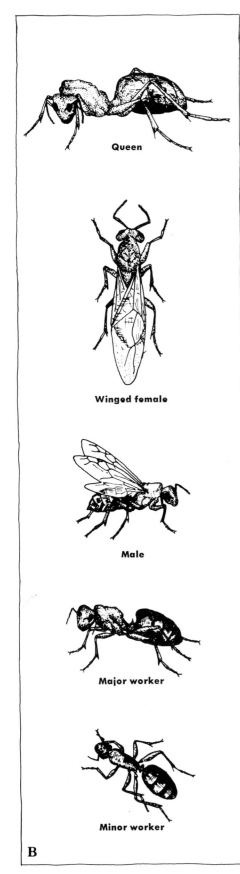

Queen

Winged female

Male

Major worker

Minor worker

B

Figure B: Some of the ants found within a single nest. The queen is the largest.

Facts about Ants

An ant's body is divided into three segments, the head, the thorax, and the abdomen, which are usually visible to the naked eye. See figure C. To see these segments on tiny ants, however, you will need a magnifying glass. The head is connected to the thorax by a skinny neck. The thorax, in turn, is connected to the abdomen by the waist. Ants do not have skeletons; instead, they have rigid outer shells made of a light, tough material called chitin that protects their inner organs.

Let's examine the head. Up front are the antennae, or feelers. They seem always to be in motion. Watch one particular ant and note how it keeps waving its feelers. It uses them to feel all around an object to determine its shape and decide whether to climb over or around it. Ants usually have two eyes, but some ants have five—and some do not have any eyes at all. These blind ants literally feel their way about with their antennae. You can examine an ant's mouth with a magnifying glass. The mandibles (jaws) are usually shovel-shaped and are used for carrying bits of soil and sand, for digging and building, and for tearing off pieces of their prey. Ants use their jaws the way humans use hands.

When an ant takes a bit of food, the food passes from the mouth into the thorax and from there into a primary stomach. This is called a social stomach because it serves as a depository for food that is to be regurgitated as snacks for the other ants in the nest. We know this is so because of an experiment in which some ants were fed honey that had been stained blue. The color showed through the ants' abdomens. Ten minutes after the ants that had eaten the dyed honey entered the nest, several other ants were observed with blue bellies. The abdomens of red ants and some others contain stingers. An ant sting smarts, but much less than that of a bee, and it isn't dangerous. The abdomen is also the seat of the sex organs and of the ovaries in female ants. Not all females lay eggs;

ANT FEEDING AND CARE SCHEDULE
MONTH _____

DATE	WATER	FEED	DATE	WATER	FEED
1	X		16		X
2			17		
3		X	18		
4			19		
5			20		
6			21		
7			22	X	
8	X		23		
9			24		
10		X	25		
11			26		
12			27		
13			28		
14			29	X	
15	X		30		X
			31		

C

CAUTION: DO NOT OVERFEED

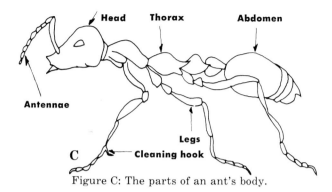

Figure C: The parts of an ant's body.

only the queen does this. The male ants' job is to mate with the queen.

From the eggs laid by the queen, larvae (immature ants) emerge. The larvae are cared for by the colony's adult ants and develop into pupae (ants in the last stage of development before becoming adults). After an incubation period, they are finally fully grown ants. A large ant is not necessarily an old one, nor is a small ant necessarily a young one.

However, in any one species—for example, one of the black ants shown on the opposite page (figure B)—there may be several sizes of ant, ranging from giant soldiers to pygmy workers. The arbitrary term soldier is given to a category of female worker ant. These are the females who swarm to form the new colony. Like the queen, after the mating, they, too, tear off their wings.

The queen is the most important member of the colony. In every species, she is larger than the other ants. In some species, she may be twice as big. You can also distinguish her by her extra-large abdomen and her three extra eyes, located between the two regular eyes.

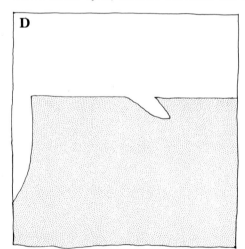

Figure D: At the end of four hours, the ants have started to excavate a small tunnel in the ant farm.

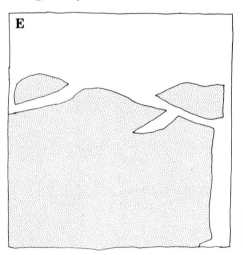

Figure E: After another four hours, a second tunnel entrance has been made not far from the first tunnel.

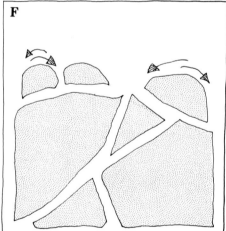

Figure F: A few days later, several more tunnels, leading to broad chambers, have been dug by the busy colony.

Ants should not be overfed, nor should they be drowned with an excess of water. Make a feeding chart (opposite) as a guide. Examine your ant farm daily, and keep a record of your observations. Ants prefer darkness, so after examining them, replace the cover. The ant farms should not be moved around, because the ants would feel the vibrations and be disturbed. You will note the ants in the Mason jar tunneled at the bottom. This farm retains moisture more evenly throughout, so the tunnels are at the top.

For related projects, see the entries "Beachcombing," "Birds and Birdhouses," and "Wildlife."

ANTIQUING FURNITURE
Refurbishing Castoffs

Rosario Capotosto, of Greenlawn, L. I., officially a photographer and unofficially a master cabinet maker, is known for the all-mahogany Volkswagen chassis he once built. He appreciates beautiful woods and the restoration of true antiques, but finds antiquing especially satisfying because "you can do so much with lesser woods and furnitures."

Like many other devotees of garage sales and country auctions, my wife and I claim to have a special talent. With few misses, we can recognize a furniture gem no matter how many coats of paint are hiding the lines and grain of the original piece. If we come upon a genuine antique (something more than 100 years old), we expect to hunt for hardware of the proper period and to care enough to make restoration parts for our new possession. Of course, a really good antique is worth all the time and trouble of a painstaking restoration.

The Victorian Look

Most of the bargain pieces found at garage sales are not fine antiques. Nevertheless, many are worth fixing up, and the results can be handsome. While you can't make or fake a real antique by the methods shown here, you can give old pieces, and even new unfinished furniture, the styling of a bygone era, as well as a feeling of age and wear, by using the time-and-patience-saving method known as antiquing, or glazing. Some of these trompe-l'oeil procedures were practiced by Victorians who could well afford the real thing. Jay Gould's estate, Lyndhurst, in Tarrytown, N.Y., had wooden posts painted to match a marble mantel (see Marbleizing, page 77), and walls painted to look like leather.

The Governor Winthrop desk on the opposite page was refurbished with a glaze finish, which enhances the period styling. Instead of removing all the layers of old paint, you merely apply a new coating.

Furniture and Refinishing
Antiquing with glaze

Materials for glazing are sold in color pairs—a base coat and a topcoat—but you can select colors separately. The usual combination consists of a light base shade and a glaze of a darker tone, such as burnt sienna, or umber with a bit of black in it for even deeper accents. Deep, strong glazes such as red and green work well, too, teamed with a neutral or softly shaded undercoat. In combination, the neutral base layer shows through the glaze and softens the total effect to a muted, mellow tone.

At the paint store, study the sample glazing panels on display before making a color choice. Take the time to read container labels carefully. Not all materials are made of the same components, and there may be differences in application techniques or drying time. Follow the manufacturer's instructions exactly. In addition, make sure that both base and glaze are the same type. Use oil base with oil glaze and latex with latex.

Prepare for Finishing

Remove all hardware, hinges, drawer pulls, and keyhole escutcheons. Take out drawers, so you can work on them separately. Wash the wood with mild soap and water; let it dry well. Rub the entire piece lightly with fine sandpaper; then wipe all surfaces with a cloth dampened in paint thinner.

Stir the base paint well, and brush it carefully onto the clean wood. Coat all exposed surfaces, including the back. Be sure to paint the edges, the sides of the drawer fronts, and the wood strips in front that support the

This desk, in Governor Winthrop style, was purchased in battered condition at a garage sale. A glaze finish in the manner of a bygone age gave it a new beauty.

drawers. Most base paint made for glazing tends to level into a smooth surface before it sets, but don't leave any skips or thin spots. Let it dry overnight.

Applying the Glaze Paint

Now you are ready for the glaze. Brush the glaze color sparingly over the area you are going to cover. Make each brushful go as far as possible before you dip the brush into the paint again. Use long strokes, and brush in the direction of the wood grain. Wait about half an hour, or just until the glaze becomes tacky. The next step is to remove a portion of the glaze so the base color shows through. There are several ways to do this.

Simulating the Grain

Run a dry brush lightly over the tacky glaze. Follow the grain of the wood, and wipe the brush on a rag after each stroke. Other methods are to wipe the tacky glaze with cheesecloth, steel wool, crumpled newspaper, or cardboard. If you are not happy about the effect you achieve with the first method you try, wipe off all the glaze with a thinner-dampened rag. Brush on a new layer, and this time try one of the other methods.

1: The first step in antiquing a glaze finish is to remove all hardware from the furniture. Save screws and bolts. Glue any loose parts, and make necessary repairs.

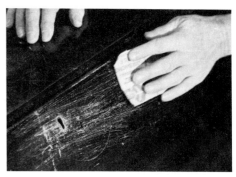

2: Lightly rub the entire piece with fine sandpaper, to roughen it so the new finish will adhere firmly. Then wipe with a cloth dampened in paint thinner.

The drawings at the left illustrate some fundamental rules for working with glaze. Wipe with the grain. When you get to the edge, wipe away from and over it, continuing your wiping stroke into the air. If you are using crumpled paper or steel wool, switch to a small, dry brush when you get to intricate areas like corners and where moldings meet. A pad of steel wool cannot fit into such places, and would make an

Wipe with the grain in long straight lines.

Wipe edges going away. This maintains the illusion of continuing grain.

Start the wipe from the corners with a dry brush continuing with steel wool.

A

Figure A: Rules for wiping tacky glaze.

3: Stir the base-coat paint thoroughly. Then brush it on in an even layer. Apply it generously, working it well into the wood. Pay special attention to corners. Brush out to avoid runs, which would show. Let the paint dry overnight.

4: After undercoat has dried, apply the color glaze. On a large piece of furniture, do one section or side at a time. Make sure all indentations as well as high spots are covered, but not flooded. Let dry about 30 minutes, until tacky.

5: When glaze has become slightly tacky, you can start to antique. The method shown here consists of running a dry brush over the tacky glaze. A cheap, coarse brush is best for this job. The objective is an evenly streaked surface.

6: Erratic fingertip pattern in set glaze.   7: Surface evenly streaked with dry brush. 8: Surface mottled with aluminum-foil wrap.

unsightly blob. Work the corner area with the brush for a couple of inches, and then continue with the steel wool.

Remember to glaze and wipe only one area at a time. With paneled furniture, work on one panel at a time. If you try to glaze too large an area at once, part of it is bound to become too dry to work on. But if this should happen, you can wipe off the glaze with a rag dampened in paint thinner, and try again—a smaller section this time.

The streaked effect this procedure gives (see photograph 7) is just one of many ways to antique with glaze.

For a shaded effect, apply glaze more sparingly in the centers of large areas like door panels and tabletops. The lightest shading should be in the form of a rough oval if the area you are working on is oblong, a circle if the area is square. The edges of a wiped-out oval or circle can be feathered evenly by lifting the cloth as you wipe or by brushing toward the center with a dry brush. The end result is the look of paint that has aged and faded.

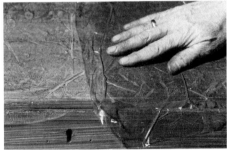

9: Shown here are ways to produce interesting antique effects. First method: Lay a sheet of aluminum foil over the glaze; press, and remove.

10: Second method: Dab fingertips in the tacky glaze, for a bird's-track effect. Do not make a regular pattern. Keep moving your fingertips around.

11: Third method: To obtain a marblelike pattern, press plastic food wrap over the tacky glaze. Smooth it with your palm, disregarding wrinkles; remove.

Photographs 6 and 8 show the textured effects achieved by using different methods to remove the excess glaze. Photograph 6 shows the result of fingertip dabbing. Bunch the fingers of one hand, and dab the tips all over the tacky glaze. Photograph 8 shows the effect of antiquing with aluminum foil. Place the foil over the tacky glaze; press it—and lift it. Patches of glaze come up with it, leaving an unusual surface pattern. Try these methods, or experiment and devise your own. See what you can do with such ordinary items as a toothbrush, a sponge, a piece of cardboard, or even a dry lettuce leaf. When you finish a section, step back and admire your work. If it is just what you want, stop; fussing might spoil it.

Furniture and Refinishing
Distressing

Distressing is a way to remove that just-made look from new furniture. Really old furniture shows the scars of use and age and often is riddled with small holes made by worms living in the trees before the trunks were cut into boards. You can't make today's furniture antique by distressing, but you can give it an antique look.

Some of the tools used for distressing furniture to give it an old and used look are shown below. The actual marks made by the tools can be seen in the photographs.

12: A bunch of nails or screws.

13: A beer-can opener.

14: A length of chain.

Distressing Tools

A bunch of nails or screws, held together with a rubber band, and a hammer are very effective for making wear marks. Hold the cluster of nails on the wood surface, and hit the heads all at once. Move the nails in a random pattern, hammering as you go. Tap lightly several times. You can always add more marks, but you won't be able to remove a mark that is too deep. Make long score marks with the tip of a beer-can opener—the scratches will look as though they had been made long ago. Beating the wood with a chain will simulate the markings of years of use and abuse.

A similar but more dramatic effect can be achieved with some large steel nuts threaded on heavy string or wire. Swung sharply at the wood, they will leave triangular indentations, as though sharp-cornered boxes had

15: A handful of metal nuts.   16: Lighted kitchen matches.

been dropped on the wood or it had been bumped in moving. For burn marks, use kitchen matches. Make a little campfire of two or three matches, and let them burn completely. (Be sure the wood has been washed first, to remove any flammable solvents that may have been used on it.)

Inexpensive unfinished pine furniture is a good subject for antiquing. The Colonial-style storage bench shown on the opposite page was unpainted when we purchased it. We distressed the chest, using the techniques shown here (photographs 12 through 16), to give the wood a worn, antique look. The staining enhances the aged appearance.

After you have distressed the smooth new wood by battering it, always check the furniture to see if joints, nails, and screws have been loosened by the pounding. If they have, tighten them, and add white glue where necessary. If nails have popped above the surface, push the protruding heads down with a nail set.

The next step is critical. First with medium-grit sandpaper, then with fine-grit and finally very-fine-grit sandpaper, smooth away much of the damage you have done. If you had bought a piece of furniture in this battered condition, you would have tried to make it look as nice as possible. Your purpose is the same here. When finished, the piece should give the impression that it has been lovingly restored. After the sanding, dust with a rag dampened with turpentine. Now you are ready to apply the stain. We used a dark walnut stain on the bench, but you can choose from many other shades, depending on the results you want. It is better to use an oil-base stain for ease in wiping the color because a wax-base stain would dry too quickly. Also, the oil-base stain is best if the surface is to be wiped and antiqued. Stir the stain well, and apply it just as it comes from the can.

◀ This "Colonial" storage bench was distressed with the implements above. Then it was sanded, stained, lacquered, and rubbed with steel wool and wax.

17: A propane torch can speed the task of making burn and scorch marks. Use a low flame, and do not hold it too long on one spot, or the wood will catch fire. Keep the torch moving.

18: When burn marks have been made, use wire brush or coarse sandpaper to remove excess charred wood. Then finish with fine sandpaper. If you wish, you can deepen the burn spots with a knife.

How to Stain

Coat the surfaces, brushing with the grain and then across it, to work the stain into the pores of the wood. Let the stain sink in for about ten minutes; then wipe off the excess with cheesecloth or a coarse rag. Pay attention to corners, where stain is likely to collect and cause color build-up. To lighten color, wipe immediately with turpentine-soaked rag. Let dry overnight; then sand with fine sandpaper. Repeat to darken tone.

Lacquering, Varnishing, or Shellacking

Shellac can be used, but lacquer and varnish are better. Don't use spray lacquer, which dries too quickly. Follow directions on can for stirring, and flow on the finish with a soft-bristled, three-inch brush. Use long, overlapping strokes. Build up several coats for best results, allowing each to dry thoroughly, then rubbing with fine steel wool before the next coat is applied. Be sure surface is free of any particles before you apply the finish. Paint stores sell slightly sticky cloths called tack rags that are designed for this job.

19: Apply stain liberally to the unfinished furniture after distressing and sanding have been completed. Raise the bench off the floor with a couple of wood blocks, and put down plenty of newspapers to catch drippings from the brush.

20: After stain has been applied (don't forget to stain back of piece), wait about ten minutes. Then, with cheesecloth or a coarse rag, wipe off all stain that has not penetrated the surface of the bench. If too light, apply more stain.

21: Let the stain dry overnight. Then, with fine sandpaper, prepare the surface for the next step—lacquering, varnishing, or shellacking, whichever you prefer. Lightly sand all surfaces, to reduce raised fibers, swollen by the stain.

Waxing and Polishing

After applying the second coat of stain, wait a few days before proceeding to this final step. Get a can of a hard paste wax and some fine steel wool. Pick up wax on a steel-wool pad, and apply to the wood with short strokes in the direction of the grain. Do not cover too large an area at one time, as the wax might dry before you could polish it. A section about 12 by 15 inches is fine. Polishing, with a rough towel or terry cloth, must be done before the wax dries hard, or it would be difficult to rub smooth and might streak. If it hardens, go over area with fresh wax, to soften the layer below.

You will find that wax in combination with fine steel wool removes the last traces of roughness and produces a satinlike finish that is a joy to run your hand over.

22: The bench was lacquered. Lacquer should be flowed on, not brushed out like paint or enamel. However, be careful about runs. Pick them up with the brush before they have time to set. A second coat of lacquer can be applied after 24 hours—longer in damp weather.

23: After second coat has dried at least 48 hours, finish the bench by rubbing it with hard wax and steel wool. Rub the wax-impregnated pad over all lacquered areas. Rub with the grain of the wood. Do one section at a time, and polish it with terry cloth before the wax dries.

Variation on a Stool

The three stools at the right started out as factory-built, unfinished furniture. Each piece was distressed in a different manner and then treated with a specific shade of stain. None of this was random. We first formed a picture in our minds of how each stool might have been used in Colonial times and then worked to carry out this idea.

We saw the small stool at the top as a milking stool from Grandpa's barn, where it would have gotten hard use and not much loving care. It was battered all over with a chain, and then the sharp edges were hacked away unevenly with a rasp (a rough file used on wood).

The stepping stool in the center would have a different type of wear pattern. We dented the seat with a bunch of nails and rasped the rungs to form flat spots found on a stool used for standing on.

If the tall stool had been pushed too close to a potbellied stove too often, it would have developed burn marks similar to the ones we made.

Finishing the Stools

All stools were sanded to smooth out the distress marks, wiped with a rag dampened with paint thinner, and then stained. Red mahogany stain was used for the top one, dark walnut for the center, and warm pine for the bottom one. After the excess stain was wiped off, no surface finish except wax was applied. The lack of a protective coat lets the wood continue its aging process naturally, and the stools will look old more quickly than they would if a layer of lacquer or varnish had been used. If the stain appears too light after it has been rubbed, let dry overnight, and then apply a second coat. End grain of the wood generally will soak up more color than flat surfaces. Recoat light areas to match.

These three stools were distressed by a variety of methods. The small stool at the top was treated to look like an old milking stool; the center one, like a household stepping stool; the tall one, like a stool from a Colonial schoolroom.

ANTIQUING CRAFTNOTES

Glaze Making

To make your own antique glaze, mix ½ inch of oil color (squeezed from a tube) with ¼ teaspoon of boiled linseed oil, and stir this into 2 ounces of paint thinner. To deepen the color, add more oil color; to lighten it, add more thinner and oil. Use bronzing liquid or gold color to add highlights and sheen. Always test on scrap wood, to make sure you have the color you really want.

Striping

Striping can add just the right finishing touch to antiqued furniture. This is best done by painting a thin line of a contrasting color along beveled edges or in crevices. Use a soft camel's-hair brush the exact width of the required line. Wait until the glaze is dry before striping. Position the piece to be striped so that you can make the stripe with a natural stroke of the hand—straight down or straight across. Striping should be done with as long a stroke as possible. When you run out of paint, overlap the new stroke a few inches from the end of the preceding one, to avoid a telltale mark.

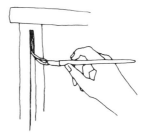

Feathering

A feather can be used to imitate the veining found in marble. Get a turkey feather, and drag it across the glaze to make a straight, thin line. Keep turning the feather and twisting it, to vary the width of the line. Keep the veining lines straight; when you do change direction, make the change at an angle, not in a curve. If you don't like the effect you have produced, all is not lost. Just wipe it off with a cloth dampened with paint thinner, and try again. Before starting veining, remove excess glaze by placing brown wrapping paper lightly over the surface and then lifting it gently.

Wiping

To get the appearance of age and wear on antiqued furniture, lighten the center area by wiping off some of the glaze with a soft cloth. Leave a darker area at the edges, in crevices, and in recessed areas. Wipe the glaze gently with a lifting stroke as you approach molding and corners. If you have taken off too much glaze, apply more, and try again.

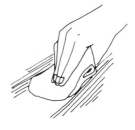

Spattering

Another method of simulating age and wear is by spattering. Wait until the glaze is thoroughly dry (at least overnight) before trying this technique. Get a brush with rather stiff bristles. Dip the tip of it lightly into the paint, no more than ⅛ inch. Flip the bristles with your forefinger to spatter the paint. To control the size of the "spats," move closer to or farther from the work surface. Spattering can be done with paint of a contrasting color or a complementary color. For example, when contrast is desired, red spattering goes well with dark gray. For complementary work, yellow spattering looks good against a brown background.

Furniture and Refinishing
Marbleizing

$ 🕐 👤 🛠️

Objects to be marbleized should be at least ¾ inch thick—as if they were real marble.

When you marbleize wood, make sure its end and edge grains are not visible, for they would destroy the illusion. To do this, fill the wood grain of the surface with wood filler or putty. Rub it in well; wipe it off. Then marbleize. Marbleizing effects are achieved by dribbling two oil-color tints over a white enamel base coat and accenting with black enamel.

Materials

You will need white enamel, black enamel, artist's oil colors (as listed specifically for the tints below), a flat brush, craft sticks, masking tape to protect untreated areas or create paint lines, and turpentine.

Mixing the Colors

Black Marble: Make Tint 1 by mixing a small amount of raw umber with white enamel and Tint 2 by mixing thalo blue, violet, and raw umber with white enamel.

Cream Marble: Mix raw sienna and raw umber with white enamel for Tint 1. Tint 2 consists of raw sienna, cadmium red, and raw umber mixed with white enamel.

Pink Marble: Make Tint 1 by mixing alizarin crimson and cadmium red with white enamel. Tint 2 consists of thalo blue, violet, and raw umber mixed with white enamel.

White Marble: Make Tint 1 by mixing raw-umber oil color with white enamel. Make Tint 2 by mixing small amounts of violet, raw umber, and thalo blue with white enamel.

Figure B: 1. Paint white enamel base on surface to be marbleized. When the coating is tacky, apply your Tint 1 by dribbling it from the end of a small stick. 2. Follow the same procedure with Tint 2, but use only half the amount. 3. Daub the surface with crumpled newspaper, continuing until the desired effect is obtained. When the paper gets soaked with paint, use a fresh wad. 4. Allow the paint to set; then dribble on a little black enamel to form a few areas and lines of deep accent. 5. Daub lightly with fresh paper. 6. Dip a small stick into white enamel, and let the paint drip off in a fine, uneven line to simulate veining.

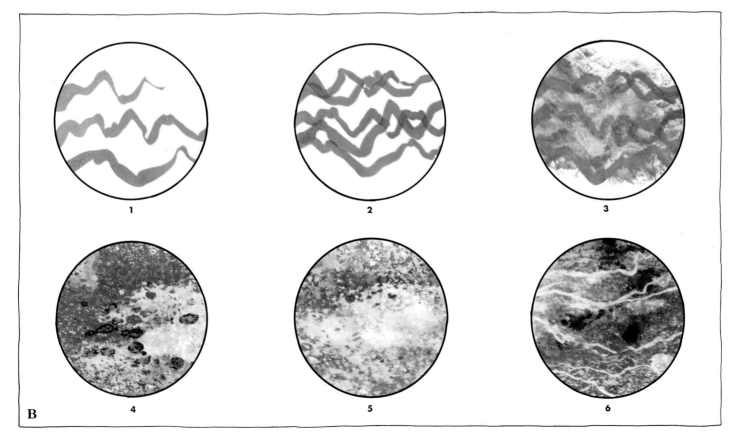

B

1   2   3

4   5   6

Furniture and Refinishing
Antiquing modern hardware

Shown in the drawings and photographs on this page are several methods for giving modern hardware an appearance of age. To simulate handmade, antique hinges, start with conventional hinges of brass—they are easier to work with than hinges of steel. Try to find hinges the approximate size of the ones you need, or just a bit larger—this means less cutting and filing. On the new hinge, use a sharp nail to scratch an outline of the shape you plan to reproduce. Clamp the hinge in a vise (see figure C). If considerable metal must be removed to create your design, use a hacksaw to cut it away. For small detailing, a file will serve. Use a file also to smooth all edges, beveling them slightly. Paint the hinge with straws from a whisk broom dipped into black enamel. These little tricks help give the hinge a handmade, worn look.

Nails are not hard to antique if you use horseshoe nails (from the nearest riding stable). These have rectangular heads made of soft metal that you can reshape with a hammer. Clamp the nail in a vise, and deform the head by pounding its four edges, to shape a sort of rosette rising to a point in the center. Nails with large heads can be restyled, too. For these, use a file to create the semipyramid shape. The modern shank will not be visible when the nail is driven home.

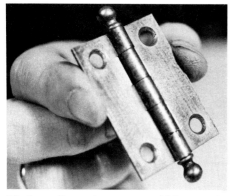

24: An ordinary brass or steel hinge such as this can be made to look like an Early American handmade one. Brass is softer than steel and is easier to work with.

25: A brass hinge shaped with a hacksaw and file and painted black. Fine sawdust sprinkled on before the paint dries (see figure C) gives it an old, worn look.

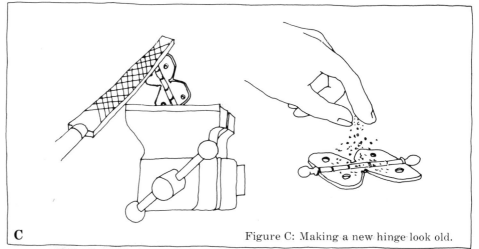

C

Figure C: Making a new hinge look old.

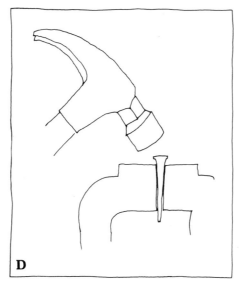

D

26: Any new nail with a flat, round head can be antiqued by filing or hammering head in an angular, irregular pattern. Place nail in vise (figure D) to do this, or nailhead can be squeezed in a vise.

Figure D: Forming nailhead into rosette.

The freshly gilded frame, with a new mat and a favorite photograph. New backing cardboard and paper, two screw eyes, and picture wire completed the renovation.

Furniture and Refinishing
Gilding the easy way

Gilding is an easy way to simulate the beauty of old gold-leaf. Paste gilding is gold-colored pigment in a waxy base. When applied to a surface, it is similar to genuine gold leaf, but not as delicate.

The frame shown here we bought for a dollar at a flea market. We wiped away the dust, then removed and discarded the covering in back, and the picture and its mat. We removed the glass and washed it carefully.

Next, we cleaned the frame thoroughly with a rag dampened with paint thinner. We bought a tube of gilding compound for less than two dollars. Squeezing out about an inch of it at a time on a rag, we rubbed it on the frame. In a few minutes, the entire frame was coated. A toothbrush worked the gilding paste into crevices. Then we rubbed and rubbed and rubbed some more until finally we had an elegant-looking frame.

For related projects and crafts, see "Boxes," "Decoupage," "Finishing and Refinishing," "Framing," "Stenciling," "Tables and Benches from Old Lumber," "Upholstery," "Woodworking."

27: This old, beat-up frame—including the picture—was bought for a dollar. The picture was of no interest, but the sturdy frame had good possibilities.

28: With a tube of commercial gilding paste and a rag, rub gilding over the entire frame. If the paste is too thick, add turpentine or paint thinner.

29: Next, use a toothbrush to work the paste into crevices. It is important to fill all cracks. Finally, wipe off excess gilding, and buff until dry.

APPLIQUE
Fabric Collage

Pauline Fischer is widely known as an artist and craftswoman, and has needlework in the collections of Colonial Williamsburg and the Metropolitan Museum of Art, among others. Author of the authoritative Bargello Magic, *she teaches in New York City, both privately and at the Embroiderer's Guild. She learned applique from her Belgian mother and grandmother. Her home is a delightful gallery of museum-quality needleworks of art.*

Applique is the art of fabric collage. The process is to stitch pieces of fabric—by hand or by machine—to a base material. The art is the picture or motif created by the appliqued scraps, and this design traditionally originates in the mind of the needleworker. Applique dates back to Europe and the Middle Ages. In Colonial America, where fabrics were precious, it flowered as nowhere else and stood as a symbol of neighborliness because so often the work was done in groups and as a gift.

Materials

Materials are the base fabric and the scraps from which the picture is created. Natural-fiber fabrics are the easiest to work with—cotton, linen, wool, and silk. Synthetics don't crease well and tend to crawl instead of staying in place while you are sewing on the pattern pieces.

Use natural or synthetic threads; I find six-strand embroidery cotton is best. Beads, ribbons, lace, and other trimmings can be added.

The tools include: Sewing scissors, embroidery needles suited to the thread selected, pincushion, thimble, tracing and carbon paper, ruler, a steam iron, and a ballpoint pen with a fine nib. For machine applique you will need a zigzag sewing machine with a special applique foot to replace the presser foot, and a can of spray glue.

Needlecrafts
Hand applique

Because handmade appliques take time and require painstaking stitches, they often become family heirlooms. To me, the work is most appealing when I have designed the motif for the applique myself. To design an applique:
□ Choose a base fabric suited to the project and select harmonizing fabric scraps from which to make the applique pieces.
□ Rough out a design on paper—your own or a copy—and cut it out.
□ Pin this pattern into place on the base fabric and adjust it, adding or subtracting elements and colors. From it make the final pattern.

These basic moves in designing an applique can vary. When I designed the tablecloth pictured on page 84, I spread an old sheet on the dining table. On it I marked the hemline, and from it worked out the dimensions of the fabric I needed. To see where an applique would show to best advantage, I set the table as for a formal dinner. Then I drew on the sheet a rough outline for the pattern free-hand with a ballpoint pen. I perfected the design. From it I made a pattern with carbon paper, then traced the pattern on cardboard.

Hand appliqued quilt blocks are for expert needlecraft artists to make. Patterns for appliqued quilts are available from catalog houses such as Stearns and Foster.

Pauline Fischer made this doll for her daughter 25 years ago. The doll pattern appears under "Dolls" in a later volume. Applique pattern for the apron is on page 85.

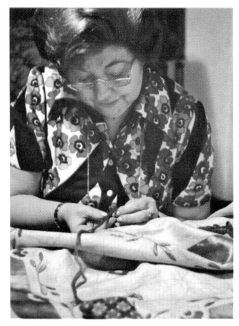

Stitching is the last step in the long process that begins with the creation of the applique design.

Applique is sewn to the base fabric with dainty little stitches of point de Paris.

In the tradition of applique, this table cloth designed and made by Pauline Fischer will remain in her family. The fabric is linen; the applique is bronze silk satin.

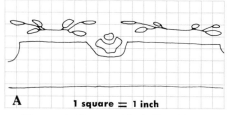

Figure A: Party tablecloth pattern.

A 1 square = 1 inch

The directions, given below, for making this tablecloth applique illustrate the basic steps in making a hand applique. The fabrics used are fine white linen, appliqued with bronze silk satin.

After you have determined the size of your cloth, following the steps described on the preceding page, enlarge pattern, figure A, (see page 57) and, on tracing paper, make a paper pattern of the design motifs.

Trace pattern pieces of the individual motifs on thin cardboard, leaving no seam allowance. Cut out the pieces of the cardboard pattern. Then trace as many motifs as needed for your cloth on the applique fabric, allowing ½-inch seam around each piece. Space the motifs on the applique fabric ½-inch apart. Cut out the motifs.

To ready a piece for appliqueing, wrap it around its cardboard pattern so that the seam allowance folds to the back. Fasten fabric at the back and catch the turned-back allowance with hand stitching so the thread goes from top to bottom and side to side. Pull fabric taut. With a moderately hot iron, press the underside. Cut free from cardboard. The seam is now pressed flat and the piece ready to applique. Snip into curved edges so they will lie flat and trim off excess allowance.

Pin the motif into place on the design outlined on the base material. Baste firmly with big stitches in thread of contrasting color.

With a single strand of embroidery thread, stitch all around the applique with point de Paris, page 86. Prepare and sew on each applique until the design is complete. Hem the cloth with point turc, page 86.

Working with Small Applique Motifs

It isn't necessary to prepare a cardboard pattern for very small applique motifs. Trace each design element directly onto the wrong side of the scrap from which it will be cut, using the paper pattern.

Designs for the doll's apron, page 83, and the bib and holder shown here, are given in figures B and C. When making the pattern pieces, add a ¼-inch seam allowance to each grid. Remember that each element of a picture must have its own pattern—the horse, the saddle, the rider. The rider's nose and mouth are executed in satin stitch, page 86.

The applique for the trains shown on the doll's apron can be made of fine cotton or linen, appliqued to a child's blouse or a doll's dress, using the basic applique procedures described above.

The bib and holder are of fine linen, appliqued with linen. To attach the seam side of the pink scallop to the bib, machine stitch the wrong side of the bib and the right side of the scallop, edges together; then press scallop to the right side.

When you applique the picture pieces to the base cloth, be sure to follow a sequence that starts with the larger bottom pieces first. For the bib, for instance, sew the horse onto the bib, and outline his jaw in point de Paris. Then sew the saddle to the horse, stitching through the base fabric; the rider is appliqued next; flowers and leaves are sewn last. Ground lines, and rider's nose and mouth, are done in satin stitch.

A generous-size appliqued bib with its own case is a perfect gift for the baby who travels. The fine details of the design will intrigue a seamstress-grandmother.

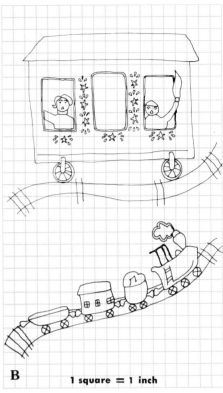

B 1 square = 1 inch

Figure B: Applique design on the apron pictured on page 83.

C 1 square = 1 inch

Figure C: Bib and holder design.

85

EMBROIDERY CRAFTNOTES

Satin stitch

Bring needle up from the wrong side at A and insert it at B. Bring needle up again next to A and reinsert it at B. Continue making smooth stitches.

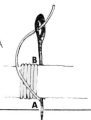

Point de Paris

1: Use a blunt needle and fine, strong thread for this stitch. Come up from the underside at A, and with the needle horizontal, stitch back from B to point A.

2: Return to B, and with the needle at an angle, come up through C, just above A. Process is the same, whether hemming, as here, or sewing.

3: Return to point A, go through at A again, and come up through point D. Point D is level with point A. This is important to note: If you go above or below A as you move forward, the openwork line will become ragged.

4: Repeat the three steps above, pulling each stitch firmly to create openwork holes.

5: The finished effect is a row of openwork holes laced by a raised ridge of fabric and thread. Fine, even stitches are essential for a neat point de Paris hem.

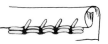

Point turc

1: Use a blunt needle and fine, strong thread for this stitch, too. As you work, pull each stitch firmly to open holes in fabric. From the underside, come up through A, go in at B to the right of A and above it. Come up through A.

2: Go in at B with the needle level, and come up in C. Note C is straight across from B, but left of A. Distance between these three points is equal; they form a triangle.

3: Repeat the step above, stitching from B through C again, with the needle horizontal.

4: Stitch from B through C again, with the needle still in horizontal position. You have formed a double stitch.

5: Now close the triangle by stitching through point A and coming up through the stitches at point C. The needle is slanted.

6: Return to point A and with the needle horizontal, come up at point D, level with A. D is as far from A as C is from point B.

7: Repeat the stitch from A through point D, with the needle in horizontal position.

8: Repeat the stitch from A through D, as before, with the needle set horizontally, so that a double stitch is made from A through D. Be sure to keep the needle straight. Return to step one and repeat through step eight.

9: This diagram shows the outline of the stitches. Actually the final stitching is not so spread out but looks like the drawing below.

10: Dark spaces here depict holes opened in the fabric by pulling firmly on the thread as you complete each stitch. The stitches should be so tight that they almost disappear. Developing firm, even stitches and symmetrical rows requires time and a lot of practice to achieve.

Needlecrafts
Machine applique

¢ ☒ 👤 🔬

Machine applique is faster than hand applique because the pattern pieces are glued, not basted, and machine stitched instead of hand stitched. It's a method particularly suited to bold designs. To learn the basic techniques of machine applique, study the step-by-step instructions below.

The first step in making the Charlie Chaplin applique for the denim jacket (pictured on page 89) is to draw the pattern pieces, figure D, page 88, on tracing or transfer paper. Tips that make this easier are pictured in photographs 1 through 4.

□ Select the fabrics. I used fake fur for the eyebrows and the mustache, crepe-backed satin for the hat, and the whitest possible cotton for the face. The shirt is a textured, off-white cotton.

□ Wash and dry the denim jacket, if new, and all the fabrics chosen for the applique pieces to make sure there won't be any shrinkage later. Starch and iron each piece of the applique fabric, except fake fur.

□ Transfer the pattern pieces from the tracing paper onto the fabrics and cut out the parts in silhouette, nose, eyes, and all.

□ Compose Charlie on the jacket back, playing with the pieces until you find just the look you want. This is the time to evaluate your design. Mark the positions of the smaller pattern pieces on the silhouette.

□ Decide which piece is to be stitched on in what order so you can avoid doubling or crossing stitch lines.

Margaret Cusack, a graduate of Pratt Institute in New York, designs applique that is machine-stitched for magazine covers and advertisements. The projects pictured here show her handiwork with fabric collage–and a sewing machine.

1: Keep the lines uncomplicated as you draw or enlarge the design to its final size with a fine-tipped felt pen.

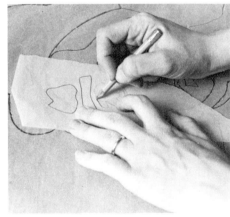

2: With transfer paper (use white on black fabric) and a pencil on a sunny window, trace overall outline on base piece.

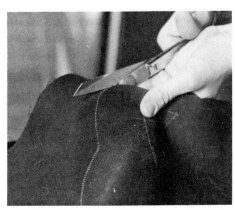

3: After applying spray glue to hold tracing paper to fabric, cut out very small shapes; peel off paper, position on base.

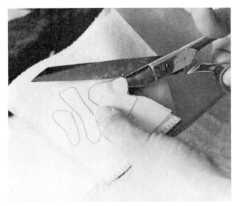

4: Using one sheet of tracing paper for all pieces to be cut from the same fabric makes transfer and cutting easy.

D   1 square = 1 inch

Figure D: Pattern for Charlie Chaplin.

5: Assembling Charlie to see how he looks before pieces are glued and then sewed onto the silhouette. This is the time to fix his facial expression.

6: Smaller pattern components are sprayed lightly with glue, face down on newspapers.

7: Glue-sprayed pieces are assembled on the cutout for the Charlie Chaplin face.

☐ Place newspapers on the floor, set the small pattern pieces face down on the papers and spray lightly with glue. Do not spray the large, background parts of the applique.

☐ Position small pieces on base fabric, face up now, and iron on.

☐ Using a satin stitch on a zigzag sewing machine with a special applique foot, sew everything to Charlie's silhouette. Iron. Spray glue on the back of the silhouette and position it on the jacket. Iron again and zigzag the silhouette edges to the jacket with satin stitch.

8: Iron at each stage of the applique to give finished work a professional look.

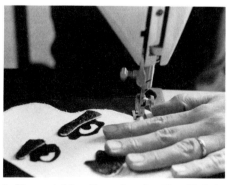

9: Use matching thread and satin stitch to sew down the components. Note eye whites.

10: Last step is to stitch the assembled design to the denim jacket back.

The machine-stitched Charlie Chaplin. The machine technique, a different approach to applique, is fast and easy.

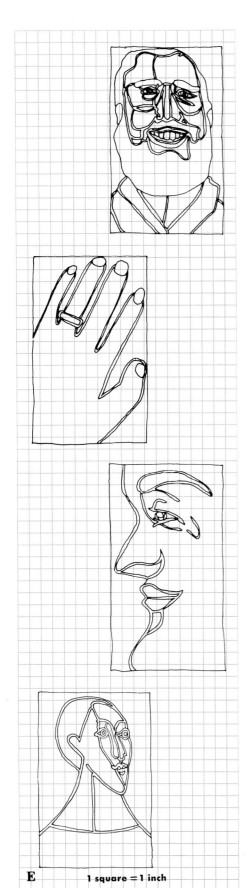

E   **1 square = 1 inch**

Figure E: Pillow patterns.

Machine-appliqued people pillows, by Margaret Cusack. Patterns for the appliqued profile pillows can be made from photostatic enlargements of snapshots.

Needlecrafts
People pillows

The machine applique techniques used to make the Charlie Chaplin jacket can be applied to make the people pillows pictured here.

The first step is to prepare a pattern. The pattern of the hand, shown in figure E, is the easiest. Enlarge the pattern on a scale of one square equals one inch and transfer the design, as described on page 57. Next, from a sturdy fabric such a closely woven cotton, cut front and back pillow casing pieces of equal size. Including seams, these will be about 11 by 14 inches and 14 by 20 inches. The dimensions aren't critical.

Machine applique the pieces to the pillow front, as explained in the Charlie Chaplin design instructions; then, with the pieces inside out, sew the casings together across the top and down two sides of the 1-inch seam allowances. Turn to right side, slip over a pillow, tuck in rough open ends and hand sew.

Make a pillow applique of a friend's profile from a photograph enlarged by a photostat shop to 9 by 12 inches. Trace the profile onto pattern tracing paper and proceed as above. Use polished cotton for flesh areas, fake fur or shiny fabrics for hair and beard, discarded clothing for garment pieces.

APPLIQUE

Needlecrafts
Applique a centerpiece

My own design of flowers and leaves allows center space for candlesticks in this machine-stitched-applique cloth. Copy this design exactly (figure F), or plan your own color scheme to complement your china. Follow the basics of the Chaplin machine-stitched applique to make your tablecloth.

More Applique Tablecloth Ideas

For the way to approach tablecloth design, see Pauline Fischer's suggestions on page 82. Unless you are appliqueing a tablecloth that will be cherished for generations and taken out for only the most formal or festive occasions in your home, use materials that can be machine-washed. Silk, for example, is suitable only for careful hand-laundering. Linen on linen, stitched with cotton or linen embroidery thread, is quite durable when machine-laundered at a moderate temperature. Organdy, another suitable material, works into an exquisite cloth. Because of organdy's transparent quality, you can applique it on the underside, so the applique shows through in a shadow effect. Synthetics are difficult to use.

For more design ideas, see Master Pattern section, Index Volume.

For related projects and crafts, see "Crewel," "Embroidery," "Granny squares," "Needlepoint," "Patchwork," "Quilting."

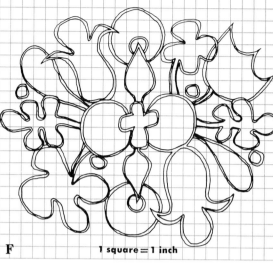

F 1 square = 1 inch

Figure F: Tablecloth centerpiece pattern.

▼ This tablecloth by Margaret Cusack is machine-appliqued. Glue or pin parts in place, then machine-sew to the cloth.

ASTRONOMY

Finding the Stars

Isaac Asimov, formerly associate professor of biochemistry at Boston University School of Medicine, is one of today's most prolific and versatile writers. The remarkable list of over 125 books bearing his name includes fiction, mystery, history, geography, and the science fiction for which he is famous. Among weightier tomes are Asimov's Guide to the Bible *and* Asimov's Guide to Shakespeare, *each in two volumes. Dr. Asimov lives in New York City surrounded by a thousand reference books.*

Since his appearance on earth, man has been fascinated by the enormity of the heavens and the enigma of those shining points of light that make a glory of the nighttime sky. Through the ages he has struggled to solve its mysteries and to use the information his observations of it have brought him. It is believed that man related the phases of the moon to his planting times at the beginnings of agriculture—about 10,000 B.C. We know that stars have guided travellers through desert wastes and over the seas since man first began to explore his planet.

Early man did not have the faintest concept of how vast the celestial vault was. Nor did he guess that in relative size his planet was not more than a pinprick of dirt revolving around a ball of fiery gases, and that this sun was only a lesser star at the outer edge of a whole galaxy of stars. It would have boggled his mind to visualize that his galaxy, the Milky Way, has over 100 billion stars, is 100,000 light years across, and is only one of an estimated billion galaxies in the universe, some of them expanding away from us at a rate four-fifths the speed of light.

But he knew something extraordinary existed up there and to fill his need to relate to it, concluded that gods peopled the skies and controlled human destinies. No wonder, then, that astronomy and astrology were once a single scientific discipline, and the world's oldest.

As long as 5,000 years ago, the Mesopotamians kept the first organized astronomical and astrological records. About 4,000 years ago the Egyptians, with the aid of astronomical phenomena, evolved the beginnings of our calendar: their year of 12 months, each with 30 days, had five days left over at the end. A succession of 36 bright stars, whose risings were ten days apart, were conceived of as spirits who ruled during that period. These divisions subsequently became the Zodiac. In the fourth century B.C., the Greeks, working with geometry as a tool, refined astronomy and renamed the constellations for their own gods and mythological characters. Today we still use those Greek names.

Although the early astrologers attributed occult powers to the stars in controlling human destiny and earthly happenings, the truths that modern science has revealed about cosmic events are more overwhelming than fiction. For instance, the faint nebulosity in the constellation of Andromeda—assumed to be merely clouds—is, in reality, billions of stars in a galaxy larger than our own. On the following pages, you will learn how to find Andromeda and other constellations from your backyard or rooftop. On pages 101 to 105 there are instructions for making a simple telescope.

A medieval artist's view of infinity exhibits a fantasy far different from the actual magnitude of the Universe. He depicts Man, Earth, the planets, the Sun, and the stars, as circumscribed in a finite circle beyond which lies an indefinable machinery that runs the Universe.

The Great Nebula in Andromeda, shown here photographed through the Hale Observatory telescope, is the most dramatic object in the sky that can be seen by the unaided eye. It is actually a galaxy, larger than our Milky Way, made up of billions of stars whose light is reaching us more than two million years after leaving Andromeda.

The charts on these pages show the night sky in the Northern Hemisphere at four different periods of the year. The colored area in each chart indicates the rotation of the Big Dipper around the North Celestial Pole. We have used the Dipper as an orientation point to find our way about the sky. The Dipper makes this same circle nightly since it is always above the horizon. Here, the January sky.

The Big Dipper and Polaris

On any night of the year, if you live in the United States, you will see somewhere in the northern part of the sky the seven bright stars that make up the Big Dipper (Ursa Major), the best-known star group, or constellation. Four stars, arranged in a slightly uneven rectangle, make the bowl of the dipper. The other three stars, in a bent line, make the handle.

If you watched the Big Dipper all night, you would see that it seems to move in a large circle around a point in the sky. Actually, the whole sky seems to move because the Earth is rotating. This becomes obvious if you watch the Dipper.

Sometimes it is seen right side up. Sometimes it is tipped on its bowl, sometimes on its handle; sometimes upside down—but it is always above the horizon.

This means it is always visible on cloudless nights and is always in the northern region of the sky. That may have been mankind's first great astronomical discovery.

The Phoenicians were the first people who dared strike boldly across the Mediterranean and explore it from end to end. They were the first to make their way through tne Strait of Gibraltar into the Atlantic Ocean—perhaps guided by the Big Dipper.

The Dipper's seven stars have Arabic names, because the Arabs were

In April, in our sky, the stars have assumed the position shown on the April Chart. Polaris, the North Star, seems to remain stationary as the Earth turns. You do not need a compass on a starry night to find your direction: When you have found the North Star, you know that to your right is East, to your left West, and at your back is South. Navigators were guided for centuries by Polaris.

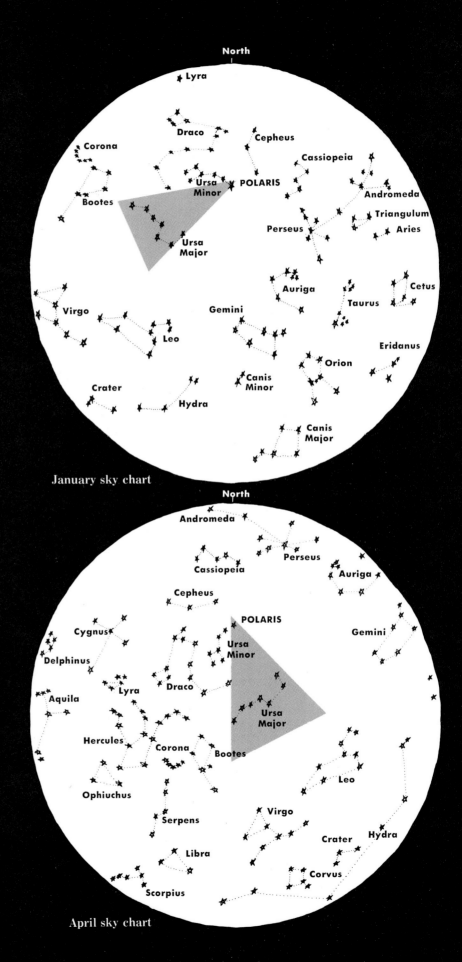

January sky chart

April sky chart

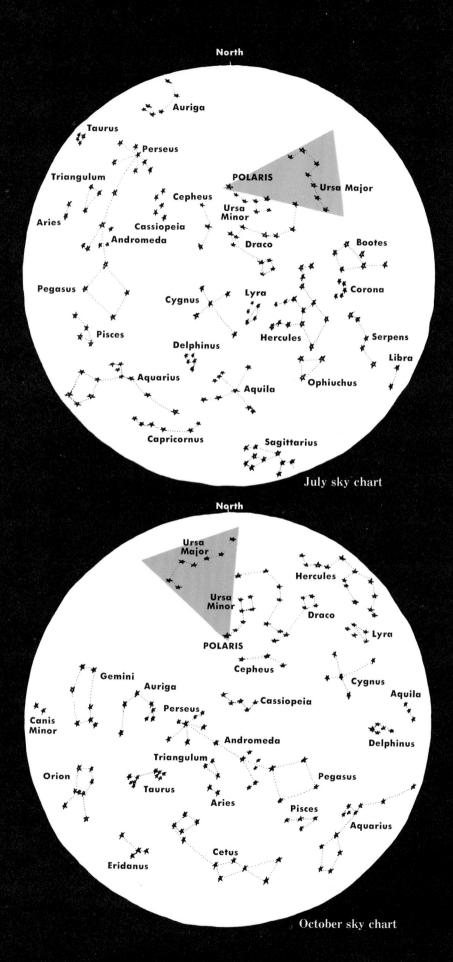

July sky chart

October sky chart

In July, still using the Dipper as our guide, we see it in the northeast. Polaris, incidentally, is the first star on the handle of the Little Dipper, also called Ursa Minor, or Little Bear. The Big Dipper is called Ursa Major, or Big Bear. Stars are classified by their brightness on a scale of 16 and the brightest are referred to as first magnitude stars. Polaris is a second magnitude star.

the great astronomers of the early Middle Ages. When western Europeans began to study astronomy again, after the Dark Ages ended about 1000 A.D., they adopted the names the Arabs had given the stars.

The middle star of the Dipper handle, for instance, is Mizar (MY-zahr), an Arab word meaning veil. Its light veils a dimmer star close by called Alcor (al-KAWR), from Arabic words meaning the weak one. Mizar and Alcor make up a double star, and it is difficult to see the dimmer one. Being able to see Alcor was proof of good eyesight. Today, city lights and dusty air make the test unfair. I have never seen Alcor, although with my glasses, my eyesight is perfect.

The two stars of the bowl opposite the Dipper handle also have Arabic names, but are commonly called the Pointers. Why? Draw an imaginary line through the two Pointers, continue it past the top of the Dipper's bowl to an area about seven times the distance between the Pointers, and you will come to another bright star. This is the North Star, Polaris (poh-LAIR-iss).

The Big Dipper, as it turns in the sky, revolves around an imaginary point called the North Celestial Pole. This point is directly over Earth's North Pole, which stands still while the Earth rotates. Earth's west-to-east rotation makes the sky appear to turn east to west,

In the October chart, the Dipper is shown having come nearly full circle around the Celestial Pole. Note that some of the constellations around the periphery go below the horizon and are not visible at all during certain times of year. While other constellations are visible at the time of year shown, they also rise and set with the Earth's westward movement so they assume different positions during the night. 95

An ancient drawing of the constellation of Cassiopeia as the Greeks imagined it to be, a mythological queen sitting in a chair. Actually, we see the five main stars as an M in the summer and a W in the winter.

Our galaxy, the Milky Way, has a spiral shape like the Andromeda Galaxy. From the side, it would look like a flat disc with a bulge at the middle. It contains 100,000 million stars (of which our Sun is one) surrounded by swirling gases. The latter are chiefly hydrogen, helium, and oxygen, plus galactic dust. Estimates place the birth of our galaxy at between 8,000 and 9,000 million years ago.

so the North Celestial Pole, like Earth's North Pole, stands still.

The North Star, being very near the North Celestial Pole, makes only a tiny circle around it. So the North Star seems to be always in the same place, and when you look at it, you are looking due north.

Cassiopeia, Alpha Centauri, and the Milky Way

If you continue the line of the Pointers past the North Star, you will come upon five bright stars a little to one side of the line. They make up the constellation Cassiopeia (KAS-ee-oh-PEE-uh), named after a queen in Greek mythology.

The Greeks imagined that stars formed groups resembling human beings, animals, or objects. These imaginary pictures were highly fanciful, and it isn't worthwhile to try to figure them out. The Greeks pictured Cassiopeia, for instance, as a woman sitting in a chair. For us, it is more useful to see the constellation as five stars in the shape of the letters W or M.

Cassiopeia is always on the side of the North Star opposite the Big Dipper, and both turn and turn and turn around the North Celestial Pole without ever setting below our horizon.

Imagine a line extending from Cassiopeia down to the Earth, through the Earth, and out on the other side of our planet, where that line would point to a bright star called Alpha Centauri (AL-fuh-sen-TAW-ree).

Alpha Centauri is the third brightest star and also the closest star other than our Sun, only 25 trillion miles away. (That doesn't sound close, but all the other stars are much farther away.)

Since, as seen from the United States, Cassiopeia is always above the horizon, Alpha Centauri, on the opposite side of the sky, is always below the horizon. The ancient Greeks and medieval Arabs never saw Alpha Centauri, and we can't either unless we travel south to the tropics or, for a really good view, to Argentina or South Africa.

Imagine, though, that we are living on a planet circling Alpha Centauri. Most of the stars are so distant that a shift of our eyes from here to Alpha Centauri is too small a change to make any significant difference. The stars would still make the same patterns in the sky—with one important exception. Cassiopeia would contain not five stars in a zigzag line, but six, and the sixth star would be our Sun.

If you were out in the country, with no lights anywhere, and if the sky were cloudless, clear, and moonless, you would see a dim, shining band passing through Cassiopeia. You could follow that band toward the horizon in either direction. This is the Milky Way.

The ancients never knew what the Milky Way is; but the telescope has proved it to be composed of myriads of very faint, very distant stars. This whole system of stars is shaped like a huge lens. When we look through the long axis of the lens, the innumerable stars we see for trillions of miles merge to form a luminous fog.

Star Groups

The Big Dipper and Cassiopeia are examples of star groups that never set and are always in the sky. Star groups farther from the North Star make such big circles that they move beyond the horizon. They rise and set, so they are above the horizon and visible only part of the time.

The Earth's rotation makes the Sun seem to change its position slowly against the stars, so that it appears to complete a circuit of the sky in one year. So the star groups rise and set above the horizon during the daytime for half the year and above the horizon during the nighttime the other half. Sunlight, of course, blots out the stars during the day.

As nights are longer in winter and the air tends to be clearer on cold nights, star-hunting is most successful late on a winter night. As it happens, the star groups visible in the night sky when it is winter in the Northern Hemisphere are particularly beautiful. On the following pages we will describe how to find some of these groups.

This Great Nebula in Orion is located in the Giant's belt. A cloud of hydrogen and dust, it also includes some hot stars and looks green because of oxygen emissions.

Orion

The most beautiful of all the constellations is Orion (oh-RYE-on). Orion was a giant hunter in Greek mythology, and in this constellation we can almost see the picture the Greeks imagined. At its center are three bright stars, closely spaced in a straight line. This is Orion's belt. Above the belt are two stars representing the hunter's shoulders; below the belt are two stars representing his feet. (Somewhat dimmer stars represent a club in one hand, a shield in the other.)

The brighter shoulder star is a first-magnitude star (the twenty brightest stars are of the first magnitude) named Betelgeuse (BEE-tul-jooz). You may be able to discern that it is reddish in color.

Betelgeuse is a red giant. It is a cool star, with a surface that is not very hot or bright, and it would be dim indeed if it were merely the size of the Sun. It is, however, between 300 and 400 times wider than the Sun, and it pulsates, growing larger and smaller like a beating heart. At its largest, it is 350 million miles across. If Betelgeuse were in the Sun's place, it would fill the space through which Earth passes.

The brighter of the two stars below Orion's belt is another star of the first magnitude, named Rigel (RYE-jel). Though smaller than Betelgeuse, it is far brighter—about 16,000 times brighter than our Sun would be if both were seen from the same distance.

If Rigel were where the Sun is, Earth's oceans would boil away and its crust would grow red-hot. We would have to travel way out to the planet Uranus to find bearable temperatures.

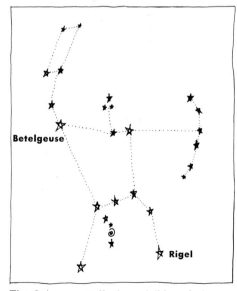

The Orion constellation, visible only in the winter sky, is seen as a giant hunter with a club and a shield. Two stars of the first magnitude make the constellation easy to find: Betelgeuse on his right shoulder and Rigel in his left foot. Betelgeuse is so huge (500 times as big as our Sun and 17,000 times brighter) that it is the ninth brightest star in our sky.

▼ This group of stars, called the Pleiades, is found near Taurus. The stars were named the Seven Sisters because at one time seven could be seen. Today, because of pollution, we rarely can see more than six. Studies with telescopes indicate there may be as many as 50 stars in the total cluster. The bright blue light they emit shows they are young stars.

▼ Right: Jupiter, which shows as one of the brightest white stars in the sky, is also the largest planet in our solar system. It has a diameter 11 times that of Earth, almost the size of a small star. With the aid of a telescope we can see the shifting parallel cloud bands. The round object, called the Red Spot, has puzzled astronomers for years. It is variously thought to be a floating meteor or a topographical feature.

At a right angle to Orion's belt are three dimmer stars, which form his sword. The middle star looks hazy, for you see not only a star but a patch of dust and gas called a nebula (NEB-yoo-luh), the Latin word for cloud. Through a telescope, this tiny patch becomes the Great Orion Nebula, pictured on page 97, a vast, foggy cloud containing enough dust and gas to make 10,000 stars the size of the Sun. The Great Orion Nebula glows because it is heated by the radiant energy of nearby stars.

Sirius, the Dog Star

If you concentrate on Rigel and the other star making Orion's feet and then look left of them, you will come upon a star that shines like a diamond. This is Sirius (SIH-ree-us), the brightest star of all. It is bright partly because it really is bright, 26 times as luminous as our Sun, and partly because it is close. Of all the stars we can see over the United States, Sirius is the closest, only 50 trillion miles

The Crab Nebula in Taurus is believed to be the result of a supernova chronicled by Chinese and Japanese astronomers in 1054 A.D., so bright that it was visible in the daytime for 23 days. A supernova is an extremely bright star that explodes, leaving an enormous swirl of stars and fast-moving gases expanding outward. The inner light of the nebula is caused by electrons which are moving with speeds close to that of light within a strong magnetic field. Enormously hot stars also serve to light up the nebula.

away. It takes a beam of light one year to travel nearly six trillion miles, so light from Sirius takes eight and a half years to reach us; for that reason, we say Sirius is eight and a half light-years away.

The only bright star closer than Sirius is Alpha Centauri, which is four and one-third light-years away. It is not visible from the United States. Three other stars are known to be closer than Sirius, but they are very tiny and dim and can be seen only with a telescope.

Sirius is called the Dog Star because it is part of a constellation the Greeks visualized as a dog. Because Sirius is so bright, they thought it must give off heat. In the summer, when Sirius is above the horizon in the daytime, and invisible, the Greeks believed that its heat, added to the Sun's heat, made the temperature very high. (That is why we still talk of the dog days of midsummer.) Of course, this is just a legend. Sirius does not give off any perceptible heat.

Taurus, the Pleiades, and the Planets

If you look on the side of Orion opposite Sirius, you will see another bright star, Aldebaran (al-DEB-uh-ran), part of a V-shaped group of stars forming the constellation Taurus (TAW-rus). The Greeks pictured Taurus as a bull, with Aldebaran marking one eye.

Now look beyond Aldebaran on the side opposite Orion, and you will see a small group of dim stars. There are six (some people can see seven). These are the Pleiades (PLEE-uh-deez), the most remarkable cluster of stars visible to the unaided eye. With a telescope, you can see hundreds of stars in Pleiades. With the eye alone, you see only the six brightest.

Other bright "stars" visible in the sky are not stars at all but planets which shine only by light reflected from the Sun; but they are so close to us that they appear to shine more brightly than the stars. The planets were called wanderers by the ancients because, as they circle the Sun in their separate orbits, they do not maintain fixed positions. However, if you see a very bright "star" in the west soon after sunset when no other stars are visible, it is surely the planet Venus. Venus is brighter than any star and can be ten times as bright as even Sirius.

A very bright "star" high in the sky later at night is likely to be the planet Jupiter as it orbits the Sun—measured in Earth-time—every 12 years. It is easily distinguished from Mars because Mars looks red.

Perseus and Andromeda

Look at the sky between Taurus and Cassiopeia. The stars in that area make up the constellation Perseus (PUR-syoos), which contains two bright stars. The one closer to Taurus is Algol (AL-gol).

Algol is most unusual; it is a variable star, the most noticeable one in the sky. Every three days, it loses about two-thirds of its brightness over a five-hour period, then regains it in the next five hours. It behaves this way because a dim star circles it and every three days gets in front of Algol and eclipses it.

To the ancient Greeks, this seemed most mysterious. Perseus, in the Greek myth, killed Medusa, the Gorgon whose appearance was so frightful that men who looked at her were turned to stone. The Greeks pictured Algol as representing Medusa's head, carried by Perseus. Algol

Stonehenge, on Salisbury Plain in England, once thought of as a Stone Age pagan temple, now is believed to be one of Earth's oldest astronomical observatories, predating even Mesopotamian works. Archeological studies show Stonehenge was built in three stages over several hundred years. The original work consisted of the outer circle of 56 equidistant holes (plus mounds and ditches) called the Aubrey holes after their discoverer, John Aubrey. Beyond the outer circle is the heelstone: the day on which the Sun rises over the heelstone marks midsummer–June 21. Next was erected the middle circle of bluestone blocks called the Sarsen circle. The great trilithons, whose 30-ton stones form the heart of Stonehenge, were placed in the final building stage. Each phase of construction, though centuries apart, did not interfere with the other phases; rather, each aligns with a set of sightings geared to important Sun and Moon risings and settings, probably used to predict eclipses and mark seasons. For instance, it is believed by Sir Fred Hoyle, British cosmologist, that the geometrically placed Aubrey holes were a counting device used over a 56-year period to mark the 18.61-year lunar cycle and which would have predicted eclipses of the Sun and Moon.

One of the great men of astronomy, Galileo Galilei, Italian mathematician, astronomer, and physicist. He was the first man to view the stars through a telescope and so began a new epoch in astronomy.

Illustration of the Zodiac entitled "The Astrologer and Fortune Teller" from an old Hungarian *Gypsy Planet and Dream Book*.

is Arabic for the ghoul. For these reasons, Algol is called the Demon Star, although there is nothing demonic about it. Let me direct your eyes to one more object. Draw a line from the North Star to the middle star of Cassiopeia, and keep going. The group of stars you will see just beyond Cassiopeia forms the constellation Andromeda (an-DROM-uh-duh).

In the part of Andromeda nearest Cassiopeia is a curved line of five medium-bright stars. Near the center star is a tiny, hazy patch you might just barely make out on a very dark, very clear, moonless night. This is the Andromeda Nebula.

If you can see it, take a good look, for it is the most remarkable object you can see with your unaided eye. It is not really a nebula, not a cloud of dust and gas, but is, instead, a collection of 200 billion stars. It looks like a patch of fog because it is so distant—2,300,000 light-years away—and is the very farthest object you can see. Actually, this is the Andromeda Galaxy, which is larger than our entire Milky Way. Just think, that faint light we see today was emitted from those billions of stars long before man walked the Earth.

The Zodiac

Taurus is one of the 12 constellations of the Zodiac (ZOH-dee-ak), a band of star groupings that seem to encircle our sky. The Sun's positions during the year place it in the area of each constellation for one month.

Not all the Zodiac constellations are as noticeable as Taurus. One visible in the winter sky is Gemini (JEM-in-nee), or the Twins. If you draw an imaginary line through Orion from Rigel up through Betelgeuse and beyond, you will come to two bright stars close together. These are Castor (KAS-tor) and Pollux (POL-uks), named for the famous twins in Greek mythology. The Moon and our various planets are also to be found somewhere among the constellations of the Zodiac.

The signs of the Zodiac were treated with great reverence in ancient history. Early astronomers observed that the planets wandered about the sky, while the other stars were fixed in their rotating positions in the firmament. They could only see five planets: Mercury, Venus, Mars, Jupiter, and Saturn. (The other planets were discovered after improved telescopes came into use: Uranus in 1781 and Neptune in 1836. It was not until the advent of more sophisticated photographic telescopes that Pluto was actually found in 1930, although its existence had been previously suspected.)

Having established the planets as such, they then observed that these bodies seemed to travel through only 12 of the constellations. Perhaps the convenience of being able to assign one constellation to each month played a part in attaching occult significance to them. (Through the centuries these constellations have shifted so that they no longer divide up as neatly as when astrologers first began to use them.)

In most ancient cultures, astronomers and astrologers were the same person. Among the Babylonians, they were priests who were consulted by rulers before any important step was taken—such as when it would be auspicious to start a war. (Centuries later, Hitler depended on astrological guidance.) As man moved toward greater scientific understanding, his superstitions waned. Finally, in the first Christian century, a separation was decreed by Church authorities between the occult beliefs of astrology and the science of astronomy.

But in the eighth century, Charlemagne revived the use of astrology; the Moorish invasion of Europe reinforced its use; and its influence held sway into the Renaissance and the Reformation. In the thirteenth century, no less illustrious a Church figure than Thomas Aquinas was alleged to have used a modified form of astrological concepts in Christian philosophy, as did Dante. Great astronomers from Hipparchus through Ptolemy, Tycho Brahe, Copernicus, and Kepler reportedly practiced both astrology and astronomy. Kepler cast horoscopes, though he is said to have resented the time taken away from his astronomical pursuits.

Environmental Projects
Building a telescope

$$ 🎞 👫 🔭

The invention of the telescope in 1608 generally is attributed to a spectacle maker in Holland named Jan Lippershey. There is a story that one day, being a permissive father, he allowed his children to play with several lenses. The children came running indoors to tell him they had "brought the church steeple near." They accidentally had lined up two lenses a foot or so apart. It is to his credit that he immediately recognized the possibilities of this chance discovery. He mounted lenses in a single tube, and went on to develop binoculars.

Shortly after Galileo heard of the invention, he made his own telescope. It was, of course, a crude one, but he learned to improve the grinding and polishing of the lenses, and with this simple instrument he was the first astronomer to see four of the satellites of Jupiter, the spots on the Sun, the phases of Venus, and the configurations on the Moon. From that period on, astronomers made longer and longer telescopes because longer tubes eliminated some of the distortion caused by primitive glass. Telescopes of that day were very complicated (and sometimes dangerous) affairs operated with pulleys and from platforms. Later aerial telescopes, which required no tube at all, were used.

Then, Isaac Newton invented the reflecting telescope (the kind you will learn to make here) in which the quality of the glass was not as critical, so astronomers turned their attention to improving this kind. Today astronomers work with many kinds of telescopes. However, even the famous Hale photographic telescope at Mount Palomar uses this same principle of the reflecting telescope.

You can, of course, buy a telescope. But if you have some expertise with do-it-yourself projects, you will enjoy building one of your own, and the job will give you a great sense of accomplishment.

The world's largest telescope is the Hale telescope on Mt. Palomar in California, housed in its own 135-foot revolving dome. A reflector telescope, its 200-inch mirror is as large as can be achieved with current methods of controlling the glass during the critical cooling period. It is cast of Pyrex glass and weighs 14½ tons. With the telescope tube and its supporting yoke, the weight is 500 tons. Astronomers ride in its six-foot elevated cage. During the 11-year period of its making, at Corning Glass Works in New York State, almost insurmountable obstacles were encountered because of the tremendous stresses that were set up as the outside of the mirror cooled and hardened while the interior remained hot and molten. New methods had to be invented to control the cooling after some unsuccessful attempts to complete the mirror early in the project. Even then, the final mirror was seriously threatened when floods short-circuited the elaborately controlled cooling system, and when there was a nearby earthquake tremor. A hazardous cross-country trek on a special flat car was followed by the successful installation of the mirror in 1948.

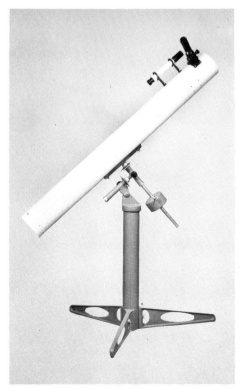

1: Professionally built reflector telescope shows eyepiece and the finder scope mounted at top of telescope tube.

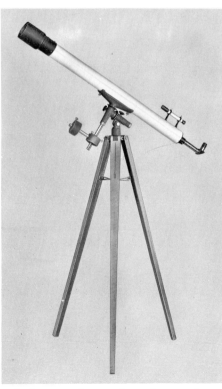

2: Refractor telescope has a lens at the top of the tube; a small prism at bottom allows operator to view from side.

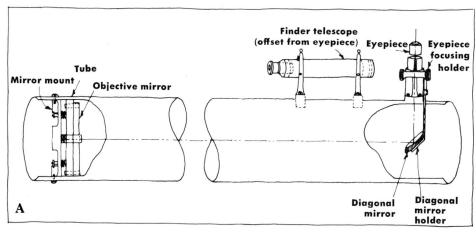

Figure A: Parts of a reflector telescope. Light enters the open end of the tube, is reflected from the objective mirror, to the diagonal mirror, to the eyepiece.

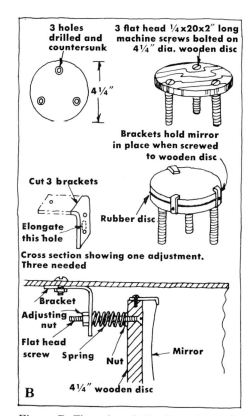

Figure B: Three long bolts through wood mounting plate are spring-loaded against brackets inside tube. By turning the adjusting nuts it is possible to align the mirror squarely in the tube.

Build your own 4¼-inch Reflector Telescope

There are two basic telescope types—refractor and reflector. A lens at the top of the telescope tube is the basis of the refractor type. A mirror at the bottom of the tube with no lens at the top is the basis of the reflector telescope. The mirror is specially ground, polished, and coated to give it exceptional light-gathering and magnification powers.

Experts rate the refractor type as slightly better than the reflector telescope of equivalent power, but the reflector scope is easier to use, and costs less to buy or to build. The telescope for this project is the reflector type, and its mirror will provide magnification of 240X to 255X—enough to allow you to observe the craters on the Moon, Saturn's rings, Jupiter's moons, double stars—even a newspaper headline up to one mile away.

Tools

Normal hand tools such as screwdriver, drill, pliers, and a small adjustable end wrench are all that are necessary for most of the work. A circular power saw is useful for cutting wood stock used on the mounting base. Other tools which will be used occasionally are fine-nosed pliers, jeweler's saw, countersink bit, tapping die, half-round file, soldering iron, and small rat-tail file.

This project is not a difficult one, but a knowledge of the use of these tools is necessary. In themselves they are not difficult to use. Careful work always produces a better job; haste is to be avoided.

Special Parts

Most of the parts you'll need are highly specialized, and it is much simpler to buy them than to attempt to make them yourself. Everything listed below can be obtained from a good optical supply firm, such as Edmund Scientific Company, Barrington, N.J.

Objective Mirror: This is the heart of your telescope, and you will need one of 4¼-inch diameter.

Telescope Tube: You will need a tube 46 inches long, with an inner diameter of 4⅞ inches. While it is possible to make your own tube by forming cardboard, brass, or aluminum around wooden discs of suitable size, it's best to order one of the custom-made tubes available from an optical supply firm.

Diagonal mirror: This is a small mirror mounted on an adjustable rod near the top of the tube. It reflects the image from the objective mirror to the eyepiece.

Eyepiece: This is the viewing mechanism for your telescope. It is mounted at the top of the telescope adjacent to the diagonal mirror.

Eyepiece Lenses: Lenses, with mounting units supplied, fit into the top of the eyepiece itself.

Finder Telescope: Because of the large magnification provided by the objective mirror, it is difficult to aim the telescope at a specific spot in the sky by using it. The finder telescope is one of modest power, about 3X to 8X, mounted on the telescope tube near the top. Use it to zero in on the area you wish to view.

Cradle: This is the bracket that mounts under the telescope tube. The counterweight assembly is attached to it.

Counterweight Assembly: The telescope must be mounted so that it pivots easily up and down, and from side to side. The counterweight assembly rides in a universal joint, and it balances the weight of the telescope so the scope will not move after it has been aimed.

Construction

Start by making up the mirror mount. This should be a rigid support, yet easily adjustable without too much pressure on the mirror. Drill three ¼-inch holes through a 4¼-inch disc of ½-inch plywood, as shown in

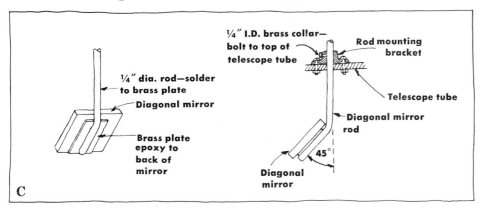

C

Figure C: The diagonal mirror holder illustrated here is a ¼-inch rod soldered to a small brass plate, which in turn is cemented to the back of the mirror.

figure B. Cut one side off each of three 1-inch angle brackets, leaving a lip of about ¼ inch. Countersink the holes in the disc, and insert a ¼ by 20 by 2-inch flat head machine screw through each. Place a 4¼-inch disc of 1/16-inch rubber on the disc, over the screw heads, and place the mirror, flat side down, on top of the rubber.

Position the brackets as shown in figure B, and

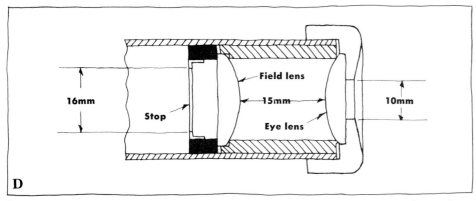

D

Figure D: Eyepiece unit mounted in upper section of sliding brass tube. Both eyepiece and finding scope are mounted on centerline, but are offset for clearance.

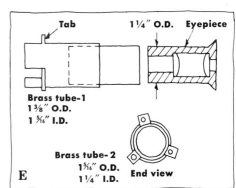

E

Figure E: Sliding sections of brass tube permit eyepiece focusing. Note how tabs are cut and bent out at bottom so unit can be bolted to the main tube. Inner surfaces of large and small tubes should be painted flat black to prevent reflections inside of tube. (I.D.=inner diameter; O.D.= outer diameter.)

mark the location of the bracket holes on the side of the wood disc. Drill pilot holes in the wood for small screws; then assemble the brackets to the disc. It's a good idea to elongate the holes in the brackets with a small rat-tail file so the lips can be adjusted snugly against the mirror.

Assemble three 1-inch brackets to the screws protruding from the wooden disc. Note that a nut goes on first, then a spring, then the bracket, and finally the adjusting nut.

Place the whole assembly inside the telescope tube, as shown in figure D, page 103, so there is ½ inch from the end of the tube and the edge of each bracket. Mark the location of the bracket holes on the tube, and drill them. Do not mount the mirror in the tube at this time.

Next, make up the diagonal mirror assembly. Cut a small square of sheet brass, slightly smaller than the size of the mirror. Bend a 3-inch piece of ¼-inch brass rod to a 45-degree angle as shown in figure C, and solder the brass square to it. Use epoxy glue to cement the back of the diagonal

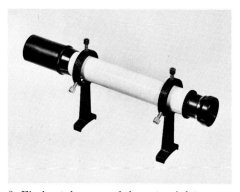

3: Finder telescope of three to eight power can be mounted on top of the tube as an aid in aiming the telescope. The main scope alone, with its power to magnify 240 to 255 times, takes in too little sky area to make it possible to locate a specific star quickly.

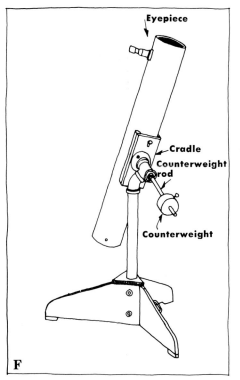

Figure F: "Equatorial" mount cradle pivots in the T section of pipe fitted to the short, curved section. Counterweight helps to keep this axis level.

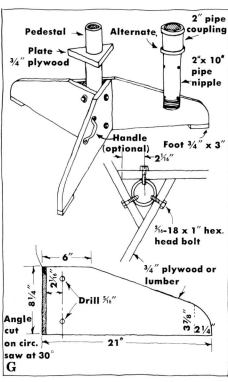

Figure G: A three-fourths-inch plate on top of base centers pipe in stand, or the legs can be bolted to pipe nipple, allowing pedestal pipe to pivot in coupling section.

mirror to the brass plate. The bend in the rod should line up with the top of the mirror.

The eyepiece consists of a focusing holder and the eyepiece lenses with their mounts. The focusing holder is made up of two telescoping sections of brass tube, each about two inches in length. Buy two tubes with outside diameters of 1⅜ inches and 1 5/16 inches. Ask for 1/32-inch wall thickness. Make three cuts across one end through the centerline of the 1⅜-inch diameter tube, ⅜ inch deep. Using fine-nosed pliers, bend out three tabs as shown in figure E. Drill a hole in each tab. Paint all interior surfaces of these tubes flat black. The eyepiece lens assembly slides into the upper end of the 1¼-inch inner diameter tube. Slide the sections together. A tight, wide rubber band at each of the slide joints will help hold the tubes in position when they are focused.

There is some variation in the focal length of objective mirrors, and the distance from this mirror to the diagonal mirror is critical. The instructions you receive with your objective mirror will give you the exact distance from the objective mirror at which you are to make holes for the diagonal mirror rod and the eyepiece focusing holder. Mark the centerpoint for each hole on the telescope tube. Drill a ¼-inch hole for the diagonal mirror rod, and cut a 1 7/16-inch hole for the eyepiece focusing holder. Mark the hole carefully, drill a pilot hole in the circumference, cut the hole with a jeweler's saw, and smooth the edges with a half-round file. With the diagonal mirror, you will receive a mounting bracket that has a thumb screw in it which allows you to adjust the mirror. Position the bracket over the ¼-inch hole, and then mark and drill the mounting holes. Do not attach units to the tube at this time.

The finder telescope is supplied with two mounting brackets, which are shown in photograph 3. This telescope mounts on the upper centerline of the tube, near its top end, as can be seen in figure A. Mark and drill the mounting holes for these brackets.

Finally, position the cradle on the bottom of the tube, at the center, and mark and drill its mounting holes.

Now paint the interior of the tube flat black. When dry, assemble the objective mirror, diagonal mirror, eyepiece, finder telescope, and cradle to the tube with machine screws or self-tapping metal screws.

Next make up the mount for the telescope. Easiest to build is the "Equatorial" mount, figure F. The basis of this mount is standard galvanized iron pipe, 1-inch inner diameter, with standard pipe fittings. The T fitting, which accepts the counterweight rod assembly, is screwed onto a 45-degree street-elbow fitting. This, in turn, screws onto a straight length of pipe that is long enough to put the eyepiece at a comfortable height when the telescope is in use.

The base of the mount is three pieces of ½-inch hardwood or plywood (exterior-grade), cut as shown in figure G. By cutting a 30-degree angle at the edge of each piece, you will get a snug fit where the edge butts against the side of the adjacent piece. Holes are drilled through board and the pipe, and the holes in the pipe are tapped to take bolts, as shown. Use 5/16-inch-18 by 1-inch coarse thread bolts.

A small triangle of wood, drilled to accept the pipe, is glued and nailed to the three legs. The entire unit is strong, sturdy, and free of vibration. Legs can be disassembled from the pipe by removing the bolts, and the counterweight rod assembly can be unscrewed from the bottom of the telescope, for storage.

An alternate method is to mount permanently a short length of pipe (a pipe nipple) to the base, and use a pipe coupling to attach the main pipe. The base removes in one piece. The details of this assembly also are shown in figure G.

Aligning and Adjusting your Telescope

After assembling the telescope, aim it up toward a bright light, or the daylight sky. Remove the lens unit from the eyepiece, and look through the eyepiece holder. Adjust the diagonal mirror until it is centered in the diagonal mirror. This is shown as figure H.

Now set the telescope so the tube is horizontal, and look down the open end from about five feet away. Get in a position where you see the diagonal mirror centered in front of the objective mirror. Now have an assistant turn the adjusting nuts on the objective mirror, at the bottom of the tube, until the reflection of the diagonal mirror is centered both in the objective mirror and around the actual diagonal mirror. This process is called collimation (light alignment), and it should be checked by repeating all the steps.

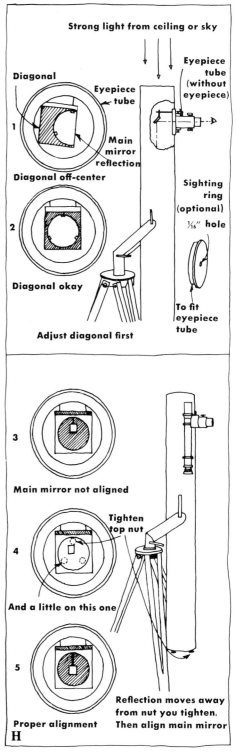

Figure H: First look through eyepiece to center diagonal mirror in the aperture and the image of the main mirror in the diagonal (top). Next look into the open end of the tube from 5 feet away, and have a friend adjust main mirror until the reflection of the diagonal is centered in the primary mirror, exactly around the diagonal mirror. This adjustment is called collimation, and it is best to turn the telescope horizontal for this operation.

BABY FOODS

Fresh Food for Baby

Preparing and cooking a baby's meals from fresh ingredients are a little less convenient than scooping the food out of a jar, but not as much as you would think. You will see what I mean when you try some of the recipes given here. The quantities are so small and the cooking is so simple that the extra time and trouble are hardly noticed in the general kitchen work involved in preparing family meals. And when the baby is a few months old, you can make his meals by blendering small portions of the fare prepared for the rest of the family. Check with your pediatrician about the age at which your baby is ready for blendered and home-prepared foods, and follow his or her advice.

You will already have in your kitchen most of the equipment needed to make food for infants. The exception might be a small food grinder, which can be purchased for very little. To turn family meals into food for an older baby, all you need is an electric blender. If you know the do's and dont's of canning and preserving, you can puree cooked fruits or vegetables in an ordinary blender and can them for use over a period of four to six weeks.

Commercial baby-food jars are the best containers to use for this purpose, because they are wide-mouthed and small. For large amounts, use canning equipment, if you have it on hand. For small amounts, use the baby's sterilizer. All the procedures you have learned for regular canning must be followed closely when you are preparing baby foods.

The fact that the whole family is sharing at least some of the same food brings everybody a little closer together. When a mother makes her own fresh baby food, and then sees the baby eat the food eagerly, she has a great sense of satisfaction.

Karen Tierney, of Sharon, Conn., grows her own vegetables and is a graduate of an adult-education course in nutrition for children. She is married to the folk singer Paul Tierney. Karen's views have been reviewed by Dr. Richard L. Saphir, Assistant Clinical Professor of Pediatrics, Mount Sinai School of Medicine, New York City.

Kitchen Favorites and Celebrations
What to feed the baby

The first suitable solid foods for small babies are generally fruits and cereals, followed a little later by egg yolks, vegetables, potatoes, and finally poultry and meat. Since fish can cause a high percentage of allergic reactions if started too early, many pediatricians suggest not starting fish until after the baby is a year old.

Fruits

The following lists give the age at which each of the popular fruits, fresh, can be introduced to most babies' diets; but your pediatrician should be consulted before any of them are offered to your infant. Babies under four months: apples, bananas (very ripe, mashed), peaches, and pears. From four to nine months: apricots, pineapple, plums, and prunes. Berries are usually not offered to small babies, because it is difficult for them to digest the seeds.

Although home-canned baby foods will last as long as any other properly canned edible, most mothers prefer to can baby foods in small batches of six or eight jars. Canning in larger batches makes for monotony in the baby's diet.

Fresh fruits and vegetables, grains, naturally dried fruits, and nuts are the building blocks for future health. Karen Tierney finds it soul satisfying to use them.

Freshly made fruit and vegetable juices are good sources of the vitamins and minerals needed for growth. Appealing drinks here are fresh apple, celery, and carrot juice.

Eric Christopher downed this blendered portion of the family's roast-beef dinner as he was being photographed. He's been eating freshly cooked baby foods since he was an infant.

Preparing Fruits

Peel; remove cores or pits; cut fruit into small pieces. Steam until soft, and then strain or puree in a blender to make a smooth texture. If the baby is several weeks old, the fruit may be sweetened with honey.

Stewing: To stew fruit, peel and core it, cut it into small pieces, and simmer it in ½ inch of water in a small covered saucepan until tender—about 15 minutes.

Poaching: Peel and core fruit, and halve or quarter it. Bring 2 cups water and 1 cup honey to simmering. Add fruit; cover; simmer 15 minutes.

Remove the fruit from the syrup, strain or puree it, and add a little water if needed to make the texture smooth. This quantity of syrup will poach about half a dozen cut-up, medium apples, pears or other small fruits. Vary the baby's diet by combining fruits—apples and pears, and pears and peaches or plums are combinations most babies enjoy.

When ready to introduce a new fruit flavor to the baby, poach 3 of a bland fruit the baby is accustomed to with a single new fruit—3 pears with 1 ripe peach, for instance. Next time, offer a mixture that is half pears and half peaches, and finally, poach and serve the peaches alone.

Cereals

Cream of wheat or cream of rice may be served alone to the baby, or combined with honey or pureed fruit. Younger babies·can be fed the bland cereals enriched with iron; those seven months or older can begin eating the whole-grain cereals rich in natural nutrients.

Eggs

As some babies have a tendency to be allergic to egg white, egg yolk is usually offered to infants first. Boil the egg 3 minutes, and mix with cereal or serve alone. A little iodized salt will improve the flavor and will not harm the baby if used in moderation. To reheat mixture, put it in a baby-food jar. Stand jar, uncovered, in a saucepan. Add boiling water to come halfway up the jar; and heat until food is just warm. Or:

Beat 4 egg yolks until creamy. Stir in 2 cups of cold, fresh chicken broth, and beat again. Simmer in a double boiler, stirring, about 20 minutes, until thickened. This custard is suitable for babies. Older

children enjoy it, too. Or:
Blend 2 hard-cooked egg yolks and a stalk of celery, with minced leaves, at Blend or Low speed. Add a few drops of vegetable oil and lemon juice, to taste. Mixture should be moist and smooth.

Vegetables

Babies under four months may be given beets, carrots, peas. From four to nine months, they may have green beans, squash, sweet potatoes. Many babies dislike mashed potatoes and strong-tasting vegetables, such as broccoli and spinach. Their first preference seems to be for the sweeter vegetables. Prepare vegetables for baby according to the directions above for fruits.

Preparing Meat

Freeze the meat for one hour. Flake the meat or chicken breast by scraping surface with a dull knife, and place meat in baby-food jars. Add enough commercial chicken broth, water, or milk to cover the meat. Stand jars, uncovered, in a saucepan of simmering water, with the water coming halfway up jars. Cover, and cook 20 minutes, until the meat has lost any trace of pink. Seal jars, allow to cool, and freeze. Do not use commercially ground meats—they contain too much fat and gristle.

Cooking Fish

Place a cup of milk in a saucepan. Add a small 4-ounce piece of fish such as flounder and ⅛ teaspoon salt. Cover, and poach for 8 minutes, until the fish is white, opaque, and flakes easily. Puree the fish in a blender, adding enough of the milk to form a smooth puree. Store extra fish in baby-food jars, and freeze until ready to use.

1: Karen cuts chunks this size for use in the blender when making fruit and vegetable juices. She washed ingredients but doesn't peel them— cores fruits such as apples. She does peel citrus fruits, and she removes seeds in all types of fruits.

2: Cut-up fruits go into juicer a chunk at a time. Top pushes fruit into juicer. When blending fruits and vegetables, push blender one through juicer first; add second in quantities to taste, the same way you use a seasoning.

3: Produce can go in whole, so long as it has been well washed. Just keep pushing the stalks down into the opening. Juices also can be made in a blender—set at Liquefy. Strain pulp from the juice.

Vegetable and Fruit Juices

Fresh, raw vegetables and fruit juices, besides being delicious, are a good way to provide natural vitamins and minerals for older babies and for children. Children raised on such natural sugars often have little taste for refined-sugar-sweetened candies and cakes. Juices may be made in the blender at Liquefy or Fast setting, or in a juicer.

One juice combination older children seem to like especially is equal parts carrot and apple juice, which are rich sources of vitamin A. Also try equal parts carrot and celery; carrot and celery with as much beet; carrot, tomato, and spinach. Melon juice is delicious. And so is pink milk, a blend of equal parts milk and carrot juice.

Karen's snack bowl for youngsters has one part dried fruit to two parts seeds and nuts. A few strawberries or cherries, in season, make the mix even more appetizing.

Kitchen Favorites and Celebrations
Breakfast cookies

It isn't always easy to interest young children in wholesome, nourishing food in the morning. One way to solve the problem is to make breakfast cookies from nuts and grains. They don't taste as sweet as commercial cookies, but they do provide much sounder nutrition. They contain honey and molasses, instead of sugar, dried fruits, whole grains, and nuts and milk for protein. A glass of milk and a handful of these cookies is a light breakfast, but it provides many of a child's daily nutritional requirements.

To make the cookies sweeter, add as much more honey as the batters can absorb without becoming liquid. The cookies take only minutes to cook, can be mixed the night before, refrigerated, and then baked in the morning.

4: Honey is the sweetener Karen prefers to use in food for children, but it is slow to pour and sticks to container sides so she measures dry ingredients first.

5: Then she measures liquids in the same cup. Next, she measures oil, if it is called for. If not called for, she rinses cup in vegetable oil.

6: Then she measures honey. Oil keeps it from sticking to sides, so it all spills out when poured, giving a full measure and leaving sides of the cup almost clean.

Blackstrap Wheat-Germ Cookies

½ cup oil
⅜ cup honey
½ cup blackstrap molasses
1 egg
1 cup whole-wheat flour

½ cup powdered milk
¼ cup milk
½ cup wheat germ
½ teaspoon salt
1 teaspoon ginger, ground

Place oil and honey in mixing bowl, and blend in all other ingredients in order listed. Drop by teaspoonfuls onto an oiled cookie sheet. Bake at 350 degrees Fahrenheit for 12 minutes. Makes 4 dozen.

Delights

½ cup honey
½ cup vegetable oil
1 egg, beaten
¼ cup milk
⅜ cup powdered milk
1 teaspoon vanilla
¼ teaspoon salt

1½ cups rolled oats
¾ cup whole-wheat flour
¼ cup wheat germ
¾ cup sesame seeds
⅜ cup coconut shreds
½ cup raisins

Measure honey and oil into a mixing bowl, and mix in the remaining ingredients in order listed. The dough will be stiff; thin it with more honey if you like. Drop by teaspoonfuls onto an oiled cookie sheet. Bake at 350 degrees Fahrenheit for 10 minutes. Makes 30.

Uncooked Peanut-Butter Cookies

½ cup peanut butter
⅝ cup sunflower-seed meal
½ cup chopped raisins
¼ cup powdered milk

½ teaspoon salt
4 tablespoons honey
Wheat germ, carob powder, or coconut shreds

Measure peanut butter into mixing bowl; blend in sunflower-seed meal, raisins, milk powder, salt, and honey. Shape into balls the size of a walnut, and roll in wheat germ, carob powder, or coconut shreds. Chill. Makes 2 dozen.

Carob is mildly sweet and reminds some people of chocolate. When I make these cookies for friends who eat organic foods, I add a tablespoonful of brewer's yeast to the mixture. The yeast has a special flavor, and you may prefer the flavor of the cookies without the yeast.

Sunflower-Seed Cookies

½ cup vegetable oil
½ cup honey
2 eggs, beaten
½ teaspoon salt

1 teaspoon vanilla
1½ cups whole-wheat flour
½ cup coconut shreds
1 cup sunflower seeds

Measure the oil into a mixing bowl, and beat in the remaining ingredients in the order listed. If dough is too thick, add a little more honey. Drop by teaspoonfuls onto oiled cookie sheet. Bake at 350 degrees Fahrenheit 10 minutes. Makes 4 dozen.

Snack Bowl

Our favorite snack for a child over four is a mixture of dried fruits, seeds and nuts. Sometimes we mix in a little fresh fruit because it looks so appetizing. I generally include equal parts of dried fruits, such as apricots, apples, pineapple, papaya, pitted prunes, dates, and figs, with twice as much of unroasted peanuts, almonds, cashews, pecans, and sesame and sunflower seeds. I add cinnamon, ginger, and other spices with a teaspoonful of each to each 3 cups of mixed fruit and nuts. For related projects and crafts, see "Ice Creams," "Marmalade, Jams, and Jellies," "Preserving and Canning."

Breakfast cookies bake in minutes. Karen suggests you mix them the night before and cook them in the morning, so children awaken to the aroma of baking sweets.

Arrange the cookies on a colorful tray, and serve with milk or fruit juice.

7: Karen's Peanut-Butter Delights, recipe for which appears at left, are shaped into balls and rolled in wheat germ, carob powder, or coconut. Easiest way to coat balls is to place them in a bowl, as here, and swing the bowl around.

BASKETRY

Ancient and Modern

Shirlee Saunders Isaacson has been associated with schools and teaching most of her adult life. Her interest in the crafts began with the instruction of young people. An expert in many craft areas, Shirlee is now associated with a crafts boutique near her Roslyn, L. I. home.

Basket making is not only one of man's oldest crafts, but one of the most universal. From Iraq to Egypt and from Europe to China, ancient basket makers were practicing their expertise long before recorded history. The Indians of this continent have been skilled basket weavers for at least 9,000 years and are considered to be among the world's most talented basket making peoples.

It is impossible to trace basketry back through time to its earliest roots because the natural-fiber materials used then, and now, are perishable. It is known, however, that basketry preceded pottery as a craft in both North and South America. Coiled baskets, described on page 115, were probably the first baskets constructed by prehistoric man.

Basket making materials are readily available and inexpensive. A one-pound hank of round cane, for instance, is about the price of two pounds of butter. The techniques of basket making are easy to master.

Glossary of terms

Hank: A one pound bundle. Basketry materials are sold by the hank.

Base: Bottom of the basket. Baskets generally are woven from the base up.

Wooden base: A flat piece of wood with holes into which are set stakes (see below) on which the basket sides are woven. See page 116 for an example of a wooden base.

Woven base: Stakes interwoven to form basket base. See page 118, photographs 16, 17 and 18.

Footing: A row of weaving worked around the base when a wooden base is used. See page 116 for an example, photograph 10.

Stakes: The canes used to make a woven base; also, those set into a base to create the framework on which the basket sides are woven.

Upsetting: Term to describe the setting of stakes into a base to form uprights on which sides are woven. These are called "upsett stakes."

Weavers: Cane, or other basketry materials, with which the sides and sometimes the base are woven.

Piecing weavers: Term used to describe the technique for working a new weaver into the basket when the previous weaver is used up. The new weaver is placed behind the stake where the previous weaver ended. Basketry materials are dampened before using to make them supple; when the basket is completed, the weavers dry and become rigid so weaver ends stay where placed. (Clip ends when basket is finished, inside, close to weaving.)

Simple weaving: Technique in which a single weaver is passed over one stake and under the next. In simple weaving, an odd number of stakes must be used. The pencil holder project, page 114, is an example of simple weaving.

Pairing: Technique in which two weavers are intertwined around each stake, then woven, one in front, one behind, each stake. See page 118, photograph 19.

Double pairing: Pairing worked with two pairs (four) weavers. Two go behind the stakes, two in front. See page 118, photograph 20.

Triple weaving: Similar to pairing, but three weavers are used, or three pairs of weavers. The bottom weaver always goes over the top weaver, so weavers are intertwined as they entwine stakes. See photograph 12, page 116, and figure B, page 116.

Waling: A strip of braided weavers, two or more, used to accent and strengthen basket work. See photographs 21 and 22, page 119.

This shopping basket offers a challenge to the basket maker because it combines three weaving techniques. Instructions for making it begin on page 118.

1: With scissors, make 13 cuts, 4½ inches deep, in a 1-quart plastic bottle from which the neck and the shoulders have been removed.

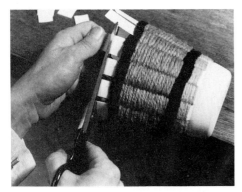

2: Weave yarn in and out of stakes, starting with end inside bottle. Weave five rounds aqua, five black, 16 green, four black. Attach colors by knotting ends.

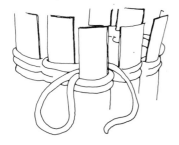

3: With scissors, round off plastic stake ends about 1 inch above the last row of weaving, which is looped and knotted.

Weaving, Braiding, Knotting
Pencil holder

This project helps the beginner in basketry to understand simple weaving, a technique basic to basket making. The basket base here is made from a 1-quart plastic bottle with sides cut to create 13 stakes. Instead of cane weavers, you work with heavy knitting worsted, 2½ yards of aqua, three of black, seven of green. To turn the bottle into a pencil holder, follow photographs 1 through 3. Sketches below show how to finish off the last row. Work figure A around each stake, draw the yarn inside the holder, knot the yarn, cut. Work yarn ends into the weaving.

To understand basic basket weaving techniques, try this easy beginner's project, fashioning a pencil holder from worsted knitting yarn and a one-quart plastic bottle.

Draw loop out between two stakes

Pass weaver end through the loop

Tug weaver end to the right; tighten loop.

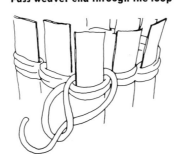
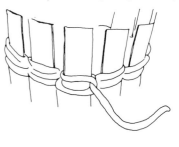

A   Figure A: Looped knots that form the last, or top, row of weaving for holder.

Weaving, Braiding, Knotting
Indian coil basket

With natural reeds and grasses, American Indians coiled storage containers for food and made a variety of useful objects, including sleeping mats and large shallow baskets, which, pitch-coated, were used as boats.

To make coil baskets, you can use grass or bundles of dry pine needles for the core and rush or marsh grass for wrapping. Gather rush in early spring, when it can be split while green and tender. Green materials shrink, so they must be dried before they can be used. For green-gray hues, dry the split rush in the shade. For brown and tan highlights, dry it in the sun. Dry grasses for about a week—pine needles even longer.

Before you attempt to make coil baskets with plant materials, practice with this easy version, using yarn for wrapping and rope for the core. Materials are about one skein each of blue and white knitting worsted; 20 feet of ½-inch rope; a tapestry needle; scissors.

Starting the base: With blue yarn threaded through the tapestry needle, stitch through the rope to make the first coil, as in photograph 4. Wind the yarn around and around the rope until an inch or so is covered.

Joining coils: Coil this yarn-wrapped inch around the beginning end, and join the two coils by looping the yarn back over the first coil twice. Change colors, as in photograph 5. Wrap an inch of rope in white, loop a joining stitch back over the previous coil. Continue wrapping and joining until a white coil has circled the blue coil. Repeat, making joining stitches at every inch point, and changing colors as each coil is circled.

Making the base: Coil and join eight rounds, side by side.

Making the sides: Coil and join five rounds, one on top of the other.

Making the handles: As you work the fifth side round, make handles by skipping joining stitches for a 6-inch span on either side of the coil: Raised, the yarn-wrapped spans become handles.

Rope and yarn make up the core and the wrapping for this coiled basket. Indian craftsmen used dry pine needles or grass for the core, rush or marsh grass for wrapping.

4: To form first coil, yarn is stitched through rope end twice, at points ¾ inch apart, then drawn tight.

5: One-inch tail of new yarn is stitched through previous yarn, then drawn forward with tail of old yarn, and wrapped.

6: Joining stitches show here as spokes of contrasting color looped back over previous coil. Make two loops at each point.

7: Basket base is made of eight rounds, coiled side by side: Five more coils, one on top of the other, form sides.

8: Basket handles are formed in top coil by leaving six yarn-wrapped spans unjoined. Raised spans become handles.

Weaving, Braiding, Knotting
Hanging basket

Handcrafted baskets woven of natural cane are remarkably sturdy. In many countries, cane basketry is still used to produce strong travel cases and saddle packs for horses and donkeys. Natural cane is used here to make a hanging basket holder for a plant.

Materials needed are one hank of No. 2 round cane for weavers and chain links; 25 10-inch stakes of No. 4 round cane; a 6-inch wooden base of 3/16-inch plywood (sold in craft shops), in which 25 holes ½ inch from the edge have been made with a ⅛-inch drill bit; needle-nose pliers. Before you begin, study these rules for working with cane.

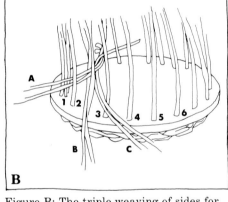

B

Figure B: The triple weaving of sides for the plant holder basket begins with the placement of three pairs of weavers, ends twisted together, inside a framework of upsett stakes. Insert two strands of weaver A between stakes 1 and 2; two strands of weaver B between stakes 2 and 3; two strands of weaver C between stakes 3 and 4. Starting with weaver A, pass A over weavers B and C, in front of stake 2, then back of stake 3 and pull it out in front of stake 4; then pass B over C and A, in front of stake 3, back of 4, pull it out in front of 5; then pass weaver C over A and B, in front of stake 4, back of stake 5, and pull it out in front of stake 6. Repeat these steps until triple weaving is completed, then clip weaver ends to one inch lengths, and tuck them inside the weaving in the interior of the basket sides.

9: Insert the 10-inch stakes through holes in the wooden base, ½ inch from the edge. Footing is woven of 4-inch stake ends protruding from bottom of base.

10: Footing is woven with basket base facing you. Pass each stake end through next three stakes, counterclockwise, under, over, under—last three into first loops.

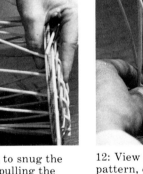

11: Turn the base sideways to snug the footing to the base, gently pulling the six-inch side stakes toward the base. Set basket upright to work woven sides.

12: View of the beginning of triple weave pattern, detailed in figure B. Three pairs of weavers are used here. Note that bottom weaver always goes over the top weaver.

13: Footing pattern in photograph 10 is repeated with tops of side canes to form basket rim, but weaving is looser and is worked clockwise.

14: Scissors are used to trim to ¼ inch all cane ends protruding from the basket rim and base, and those created when joining weavers were worked into sides.

Because a hanging basket must be strong enough to support the weight of a potted plant, it is best constructed with triple-woven cane on a wooden base.

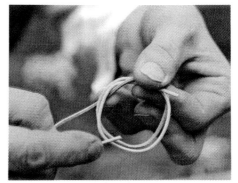

15: Links for the basket chain are made of well-moistened 18-inch weavers cut from No. 2 round cane. First link of each nine-link chain, is made by forming a 1½ inch circle at one end of the weaver, and weaving the other end back through this circle until three rounds are closely intertwined. Form the next link through the first, and repeat until nine links are joined. Make three chains, and attach them at the top with a single link, woven through the last link in each chain.

Working with natural cane: There are four important rules to remember:
□ Cane that is to be woven, pinched, or bent, must be soaked for half an hour before using, or it may crack while you are working.
□ Keep cane moist while you work by covering it with a damp towel.
□ Work with weavers of manageable length. Mine are under 4 feet.
□ Guide weavers gently and place, never yank or pull, between stakes.

Making the footing: Hold the wooden base firmly and pull each of the 25 10-inch stakes through one of the holes in the base, leaving about six inches on top, four on the bottom, as in photograph 9. Weave these four bottom-of-the-base cane tips to create the footing, as in photograph 10. Use the pliers to pinch and bend the cane if it is stiff. These maneuvers are standard when making a basket with a wooden base.

Triple-weaving the sides: Turn the base sideways and snug the footing to the base by pulling gently on the top stakes. Turn base right side up, and triple weave for ten rounds around the vertical stakes, working with three pairs of weavers of No. 2 cane cut in 4-foot lengths. See Figure B.

Making the rim: When sides are complete, make the rim by repeating the footing pattern, photograph 13, with the tops of the vertical stakes.

Attaching the chains: Three chains of cane links, shown in photograph 15, are attached to basket sides by weaving the last link of each chain through a loop in the footing row on top of the basket.

Weaving, Braiding, Knotting
Shopping basket

To make the shopping basket shown in color on page 113, you will need 31 16-inch stakes of No. 4 round cane for the sides; six 20-inch stakes and nine 10-inch stakes of No. 4 round cane for the base; a hank of No. 2 round cane for the weavers; round-nosed pliers for pinching stakes before bending. Review the rules for working with natural cane, outlined on page 117.

Starting the woven base: The first step is to tie together with wire, or string, the six 20-inch stakes at a point 6 inches from one end. Divide these six starter stakes into three pairs. Insert through them at the long end, the nine 10-inch cross stakes, as shown in photograph 16. Insert the first close to the tie and center, then space the rest about an inch apart, centering each. Around this 8-inch grid, starting at the tied end, weave 24 rounds of pairing, working with pairs of No. 2 cane in 4-foot lengths, as depicted in photographs 17 and 18.

Adding vertical stakes: The next step is to insert the vertical stakes on which the sides will be woven. Use sharp scissors to cut a tapering end on each of the 31 16-inch stakes. Insert the tapered end of each of these stakes into one of the 30 tunnels formed when you paired around the

16: Tied ends of starter stakes with two cross stakes, the first laced over, under, over; the second under, over, under. Place the seven remaining cross stakes, alternating the weaving pattern. Work the starter stakes in twos.

17: Weaving paired canes around stakes. Canes are twined around each other before entwining next stake. For three rounds, weave around each cross stake, but weave over all of the starter stakes as though they were a single unit.

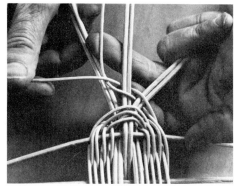

18: Separate the starter stakes into twos again, untie, work three more rounds of pairing, treating each of the three starter-stake twos as a unit this time. Separate the twos into singles; then pair for 18 complete rounds.

19: Weaving paired canes around basket sides after upsett stakes have been added to base. Pair 24 rounds, working two 4-foot lengths of No. 2 cane. Place weavers gently; never tug or pull them as you work.

20: Double pairing, working with two pairs of weavers instead of with two individual weavers. A single round of double pairing is worked after the 24 rounds of pairing have been completed on basket sides.

21: Waling, prepared in advance, is used as a single weaver and is made by braiding two or more weavers, or pairs of weavers. Waling that makes sides of this shopping basket is made by braiding three pairs.

22: Simple weave, used to work basket sides with waling, requires odd number of stakes and that's why you add the 31st upsett stake to the basket base. Weave waling in and out of stakes for 16 rounds.

starter stakes. Place the 31st stake in a center, back tunnel. This odd stake, the second in that tunnel, allows you to simple-weave the waling which forms the basket's top.

Finishing the basket bottom: Weave the protruding ends of the six starter stakes and the nine cross stakes—these ends are 3 to 4 inches long now—into the woven base by passing each, counterclockwise, over the two nearest upsett stakes and behind the third. Cut off ends.

The sides: With pliers, pinch, then bend, upsett stakes into vertical position to make framework for sides. Around this framework, with two 4-foot weavers of No. 2 cane, pair 24 rounds, then double pair one round with 4-foot weavers of No. 2 cane, photographs 19 and 20. Simple-weave 16 rounds of prepared waling, photographs 21 and 22. You will have to prepare 40 feet of waling. Follow waling rounds with two rounds of double pairing.

Finishing the basket: About 5 inches of side stake will remain after side weaving is completed. Weave these ends clockwise into a rim, working the weavers as for footing, photograph 10 and photograph 23 on this page. To make basket handles, cut two 5-foot lengths of No. 2 round cane and weave each into a ring 6 inches in diameter, using the technique for making links described on page 117. Attach each round to a basket side with a 14-inch length of No. 4 round cane. Pass the cane behind two stakes inside the basket, poke each end out through the side, as in photograph 24, loop each twice around handle, then around the nearest stake. Singe off frizzles that appear after cane dries.

For other techniques related to basketry, see: "American Indian Crafts," "Caning and Rushing," "Raffia and Straw," "Vegetable Dyes," "Weaving."

25: With a lighted match singe off frizzles that appear once the cane has dried, to give the basket a professional finish. Work quickly, or you may find you have set the basket on fire.

23: Footing weave, worked clockwise, is used to make rim of basket from the five inches remaining at the top of the upsett stakes after sides are woven. Weave last three stakes into existing loops.

24: Ends of each cane tie used to attach basket handle is pushed out through basket side, looped twice around handle, and secured to nearest stake. Ends go inside, then are snipped off.

BATIK
A Javanese Art Form

Batik is an exciting way of making a design on fabric by a technique known as wax-resist. This means that a wax pattern, applied to fabric, resists the color when the fabric is dyed. It is thought that the wax-resist method was known in China as early as the seventh or eighth century and was in use in Egypt, employing metal or wood blocks and indigo dyes, during the ninth and tenth centuries. In India, resist dyeing was known before the Christian Era. The first recorded European appearance of the method was in Germany in the seventeenth century. We think of it today as primarily an Indonesian craft. It was practiced everywhere in the Malay Peninsula and is still done in Java. Some patterns in use there were exclusive to a family and have been handed down from generation to generation for a thousand years. Tjanting, a free-form method of dripping a wax pattern from a tool of that name, was done in Java by women. The tjap—a carved wooden block mounted on copper (see page 122)—was traditionally used by men, perhaps because they carved the blocks that created the patterns.

Although I have been working with batik for years, I continue to find it both creatively fulfilling and engrossing work. I'm sure you will feel it is a satisfying hobby—one you can try with a relatively small outlay for special materials. Most of the things used in batiking are already at hand in the average household: old sheets, a small bristle painting brush, a stove (or preferably a hot plate), an iron, a candy or fat thermometer, rubber gloves, paper towels, thumbtacks, an enamel or heatproof-glass saucepan, a plastic bucket, and a supply of newspapers. You need buy only a packet of dye, some wax, and a frame. If you do any home canning, then you already have the paraffin. I suggest the table mat on page 127 as a beginning project. For that, instead of a brush you need a paper cup to make the ring design. I use this technique with new students in my classes at the Garrison Art Center in Garrison, New York. After you have made the tablemat, if the medium fascinates you too, you will want to use more professional wax and tools, and better fabrics. Following is a detailed discussion of materials that can be used. The picture at the right includes my own special tools for applying batik wax. Before you start a project, study the information below.

Materials

Fabrics: Firm, smoothly woven fabrics are the best to use, as they take the wax most easily and uniformly. An old cotton sheet (not polyester) is ideal to experiment with; new cotton fabric is harder to work with. Silk is the easiest, but I don't recommend it to beginners because of its cost. Once you're expert, you'll find it a joy to use. Coarse fabrics and those with a pile are the most difficult, because they require greater care in waxing and a second waxing on the back. However, these fabrics are especially good for wall hangings, since the different textures lend a character of their own. My own favorite fabrics are silk, linen, and wool. In general, I don't recommend synthetics; they do not take strong dyes, although they're fine for pastel shades. To be certain of finished colors, I use white fabric, although colors can provide interesting surprises. All new fabrics must be washed and ironed before you begin working, to get rid of sizing.

Wax: The wax is also important. Batik wax is a mixture of paraffin and beeswax. Neither is ideal alone. Paraffin (available at supermarkets as

Bobbi Vogel started as a painter, majored in art history at Queens College, New York, and later studied with Max Karp, now an outstanding enamelist. Mrs. Vogel found batik, originally a hobby, so engrossing that she studied in Israel with Rachael Beary. Today, Mrs. Vogel is a leading batik artist, with work in galleries, private collections, and major craft shows. She also designs textiles and teaches.

1: Top, left: Enamel saucepan containing wax, with wire for cleaning excess wax off brush; thermometer; hot plate with foil. Top, right: Japanese calligraphy brushes and house-paint bristle brush. Lower, left: Fabric-stretching frame with thumbtacks. Inside frame: Jar of dye, tjanting tools—two top ones are Javanese; the others are available at craft stores. Right of frame: Small ladle, a Japanese tjanting tool, fabric to be dyed.

Silk scarfs done in spatter or random brush patterns. The luscious colors are the result of starting with the palest dyes and progressing to the darkest.

Pictured is a tjap—a carved block mounted on a copper handle. A traditional Javanese batik tool, the tjap is dipped in wax and the pattern stamped onto the fabric.

Instructions for making this gossamer scarf are on pages 123, 124, and 125. To get the veined effect, wrinkle and crack the hardened wax during dyeing process.

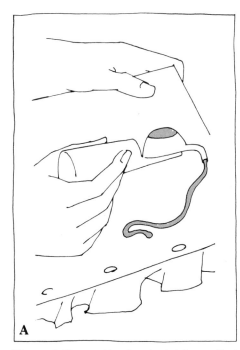

Figure A: Here a tjanting tool drips melted wax, contained in the small reservoir, onto fabric from its needlelike tip.

canning wax) is fine for an experimental project, but is too brittle for wide use. To avoid crackle with paraffin, do the dyeing in a flat, shallow pan. Undiluted beeswax is soft and does not crack; but it is costlier and will clog the tjanting tool. Batik wax is sold in craft shops. I prefer to make my own mixture—usually 60 percent beeswax to 40 percent paraffin. When I want a more crackly effect, I increase the paraffin to 60 or 70 percent. It is less dangerous to work with wax on an electric hot plate than over an open flame. Hot wax is combustible, and a thermometer is necessary to maintain a temperature between 300 and 350 degrees Fahrenheit. Be sure, too, to keep the wax away from the dye. Water causes wax to spatter. Protect the hot plate with an asbestos pad, or shield it with foil. Keep a box of baking soda or salt close by, to put out accidental fires. There's no real danger here, but take normal precautions.

Tools: The wax may be applied with brushes or with a tjanting tool. For fine brushwork, I like Japanese calligraphy brushes. They are inexpensive and flexible. Sable brushes also can be used. Spatter designs are made by loading a two-inch brush with wax and shaking it. Smaller spots are made by striking a large Japanese brush with a pencil. When doing a detailed drawing, you will need a tjanting tool. This has a reservoir you fill with wax, which then flows from the needle in a fine line. Sketch the design lightly on the fabric beforehand with a pencil.

Frame: For batik with a design painted on with either brush or tjanting, you will need to stretch your fabric tautly on a frame. You can make a frame from ¾-inch stock (see figure B), or you can buy a canvas stretcher from an art-supply store. You can also use a sturdy picture frame.

Batik with a stamped-on pattern is worked on a flat surface without a frame. To do this, see instructions for the table mat on page 127.

Dyeing: Dyeing is done in cool water; otherwise, you would melt out your pattern. Wetting the fabric before dyeing helps the dye take better. Household dyes are good, but mix these dyes, in boiling water, about triple the recommended strength. Cool the dye to lukewarm. Let the fabric stay in the dye until the shade is the intensity you're after. Remember that colors look darker when wet than when they're dry. These dyes do not need a mordant—that is, a chemical agent that sets the dye.

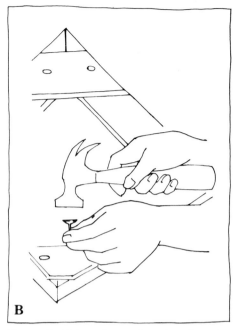

Figure B: Make a frame from four lengths of ¾-inch stock, or use a canvas stretcher.

2: Wash fabric in soap to remove sizing; dry, and iron. Thumbtack material to the frame, stretching it evenly. If project is large, wax a portion at a time.

3: Batik wax is heated in an enamel saucepan on a hot plate 300 to 350 degrees Fahrenheit. Dip paintbrush, and rub across wire to remove excess wax.

4: Apply wax to fabric in a swirling design, letting ends of brushstrokes feather off. When fabric is immersed in first dye bath, these waxed areas will remain white.

5: When wax is dry, remove scarf from frame, and immerse in blue dye bath. Leave silk in dye until it is desired color. Wet fabric looks darker than dry.

6: Rinse in a clean container under running cold water until the water is clear and no dye runs out. Stains on the sink's enamel can be cleaned off with bleach.

First dye bath

7: First dyeing tints the silk unprotected by the wax, leaving white pattern. Cracks in the wax will make random streaks of blue. Color will dry to a lighter shade.

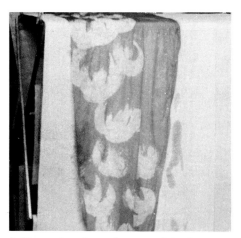

8: Hang rinsed scarf on a rack to dry. Protect the rack with sheets of paper towel to keep dye from staining the rack. Protect floor under rack with newspapers.

9: Restretch fabric on the frame when it is dry. Then paint on new wax wherever you wish. Cover any areas that are to remain blue through the next dyeing.

10: Dyes keep successfully for several weeks, but they must be strained before reuse, to remove debris. Here, rose-red for second dye bath is being strained.

If you do become absorbed in batiking, you may want to buy special batik dyes. These can be mixed as you need them and kept on hand for about a month. I use Aljo or Prochion, which are aniline dyes and require mordants. I mix one heaping tablespoonful of dye in two quarts of boiling water. (Or use one quart of boiling water, and cool it with one quart of cold.) For fabrics made of animal fibers, such as silk and wool, add two teaspoonfuls of white vinegar to two quarts of dye. For vegetable fibers, such as cotton and linen, I use one teaspoonful of salt to the two-quart mixture. Only plastic, glass, or enamel containers should be used for dyeing and for storing dyes. Wear rubber gloves, because some dyes are toxic.

Second dye bath

11: Part of the excitement of doing batik is the color combinations achieved by successive dyes. Here, exposed blue portions turn to purple in the rose-red dye bath.

12: After the second dyeing, the scarf is rinsed in clear water and hung to dry. Deliberate cracks in the wax will make red streaks on white, purple ones on blue.

13: On a pad of newspapers, iron scarf to remove wax. Paper towels cover fabric and protect it from newsprint underneath. Replace papers and towels as needed.

14: The final step is to wash the finished scarf in dry-cleaning fluid, to remove the last traces of wax. Be sure to do this in a well-ventilated room or even outdoors.

The wax is removed as shown in photograph 13. Use a plain, not a steam, iron. Remove last traces of wax with a dry-cleaning fluid—two cups are enough for a small piece. Work near an open window or outdoors. All batik should always be dry-cleaned—because of the cool dyeing, the colors are not fast.

You can follow the step-by-step directions for batiking the silk scarf. We show this project in detail because it covers all the steps for several dyeings. If it is your first attempt, start with the table mat on page 127.

You can buy batik supplies at craft art stores. Or order by mail from Craftool Co., Inc., 1421 West 240th Street, Harbor City, Cal. 90710.

Graphic Arts
Wall hangings

Exotic and exciting color combinations result from the many dyeings in more complicated batik work. The strong tones of the hanging pictured at the left required many waxings and dyeings. It is impossible in this limited space to give the waxing patterns, but we show the hanging as an example of the unlimited possibilities of the medium. It was dyed in this order: On the material, white wool, the first wax pattern was applied, then dyed rose. Waxed again, it was dyed Indian yellow, which produced orange. After the next waxing came red dye, which turned out fire-engine red. The next step used dark-brown dye, and the last step used black.

The hanging below is less complicated, and we include it here because it introduces another waxing method. Instead of being applied with the brushes and tjanting tools mentioned previously, the wax was dribbled onto the fabric from a small ladle like the one pictured in the grouping of tools on page 121. You can substitute a coffee scoop for the ladle.

Materials
Hangings require a heavier fabric than the other projects illustrated in these pages. I normally use white wool, but you can substitute any heavy material. These coarser fabrics usually need more care in waxing; but by dripping wax from the scoop, you should get an adequate layer of wax, eliminating the need for waxing on the back of the fabric. You can also batik starting with a colored fabric. You cannot be sure what the final color values will be, but the results are often interesting. If you have batches of premixed dye on hand from an earlier project, you might first experiment by dyeing test swatches of the colored fabric.

You will need a piece of white wool about 12 by 30 inches, a frame, a ladle or coffee scoop, batik wax, rose and violet dye, four pieces 18 inches long of half-round molding, glue, and brads (a type of nail).

After the wool is washed and ironed and you have sketched a design similar to ours, stretch it on the frame. Determine which areas you wish to have white, and trail the wax onto the wool there. When wax is dry, mix rose dye, and put fabric in cooled dye. Rinse, and hang to dry. Restretch. Add wax where you wish to preserve a rose pattern. Remove from the frame, mix the violet, and dye. Rinse again, and dry. Iron to remove wax, as

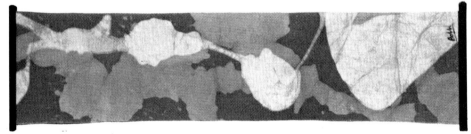

▲ To learn the techniques that make wall hangings, try the simple one shown here. The wax is applied by dribbling it from a ladle onto roughly textured fabric.

◄ Wall hanging 36 by 14 inches displays the color range of the batiking process. Originally a white wool, this hanging was dyed five times: rose, yellow, red, brown, black.

shown in photograph 13, page 125. When a solvent is not used, the batik tends to be a bit stiff from the remnants of wax; but in the case of a wall hanging, a little stiffness is desirable.

To make the fabric into a hanging, first stain the four pieces of molding. Glue them, flat sides together, on the ends of the hanging. When the glue is dry, hammer brads in from the back, for extra strength.

◀ Table mat with stamped pattern is a
good project from which to learn the basic
techniques of the batik process.
Fabric is from a discarded bed sheet.

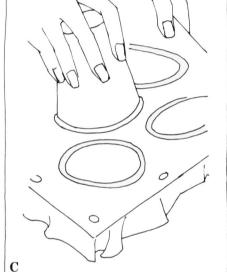

Figure C: Paper cup dipped in paraffin
serves as a stamping tool in this project.

Graphic Arts
Centerpiece table mat   ¢ 🕐 👫 🧵

In this project, the design is stamped on. You work on a flat surface
without a frame. You will need a piece of old cotton sheet about 12 by 18
inches, a slightly larger piece of waxed freezer paper, canning wax
(paraffin), a glass jar, a large glass baking dish, yellow and red dye,
newspapers to protect your work area, and a large paper cup. You can use a
cookie cutter, or substitute a can. A can will heat up as you work, so
puncture a hole in the closed end, and handle with potholders.

Spread the freezer wrap on the work surface, and put the fabric on it.
Dip the paper cup into the hot wax, and stamp the rings that will be white.
Do this at random as suits you. Redip the cup each time. When the wax is
dry, turn the fabric over, and peel off the freezer paper. Do not pull the
fabric off the paper, as this might crack the wax. Mix yellow dye in a
glass jar, and pour it into a large, flat, glass baking dish, and allow
to cool. You can use a disposable aluminum tray, but it may slightly alter
the tint of the dye. Dye fabric for about 30 minutes. Rinse, and hang to
dry. Be careful throughout not to fold or crush the wax. Next, stamp new
circles to form yellow rings. Again peel off freezer wrap. Mix red dye;
pour into pan; cool, and redye. Rinse, and hang to dry. Remove wax by
ironing between sheets of paper towels on a thick padding of newspapers.
Replace papers as needed, and iron until no trace of wax is left. The
solvent rinse is not needed. Draw threads on raw edges of mat to form a
fringe, or hem edges, as desired.

Figure D: Fabric looks like this after it has
gone through the first dye bath.

Graphic Arts
Geometric floor pillow

White linen was used to make the pillow pictured on this page, but any heavy cotton can be used. To make a pillow 18 inches square you will need two pieces of fabric 20 inches square; beige, light-golden-brown, and dark-brown dyes; heavy paper for enlarging the design; a black felt-tip pen; a pencil; a frame; batik wax; a bristle brush; a small Japanese brush or tjanting tool; a plastic bucket for dyeing; a pillow form.

First, wash both pieces of fabric, and dye them beige.

To enlarge the design: Draw one-inch squares on an 18-inch square of paper. With the felt-tip, transfer the pattern, figure E. (To enlarge a grid pattern, see Craftnotes, page 57.) Tape drawing to a window, tape pillow front over it. With a pencil, trace the design onto your fabric.

To apply batik design: Tack fabric to frame, and using the bristle brush, wax the large areas that are to remain beige. Remove from frame, and dye in the light golden brown, cracking the wax to let some of the dye seep into the beige areas. Rinse, and hang to dry. Tack on frame again. With a Japanese brush or a tjanting tool, wax geometric design to be kept light brown. With larger brush, reseal cracks in the large areas made during the light-brown dyeing. Dye dark brown. Rinse, and dry. Remove wax.

On wrong side, stitch front and back of pillow together along top and sides. Turn to right side; stuff with pillow, and stitch bottom.

For related projects and crafts, see the entries "Stenciling," "Tapestries," "Tie Dyeing," "Vegetable Dyes."

Figure E: Pattern for floor pillow. To enlarge pattern, see page 57.

Both brushes and tjanting tool were used to lay on the wax for this geometrical design. To duplicate, work with the pattern in figure E and beige-dyed cotton.